Canadian Concepts 2

Lynda Berish
Sandra Thibaudeau

Prentice-Hall Canada Inc., Scarborough, Ontario

Canadian Cataloguing in Publication Data

Berish, Lynda, 1952–
Canadian concepts 2

ISBN 0-13-117052-X

1. English language – Textbooks for second
language learners.* 2. English language – Grammar –
1950– . 3. English language – Grammar –
1950– – Problems, exercises, etc. I. Thibaudeau,
Sandra, 1943– . II. Title.

PE1128.B4 1992   428.2'4   C92-093068-9

Prentice-Hall, Inc., Englewood Cliffs, New Jersey
Prentice-Hall International, Inc., London
Prentice-Hall of Australia, Pty., Ltd., Sydney
Prentice-Hall of India Pvt., Ltd., New Delhi
Prentice-Hall of Japan, Inc., Tokyo
Prentice-Hall of Southeast Asia (Pte.) Ltd., Singapore
Editora Prentice-Hall do Brasil Ltda., Rio de Janeiro
Prentice-Hall Hispanoamericana, S.A., Mexico

ISBN 0-13-117052-X

Acquisitions editor: Marjorie Walker
Developmental editor: Linda Gorman
Production editor: Elynor Kagan
Production coordinator: Anna Orodi
Design and layout: Joseph Chin
Illustrations: June Bradford, Peter Grau
Audio cassettes: Morris Apelbaum, Silent Sound Studio, Montreal
Cover design: Aurora Di Ciaula
Cover illustration: June Bradford

    4 5 AP 96 95 94

Printed and bound in Canada by Webcom Limited

Contents

To the Teacher

The *Canadian Concepts* Series

The *Canadian Concepts* Series is a six-book series designed for students learning English in Canada. Survival topics and cultural information based on Canadian themes help students integrate into the community. These themes are recycled with increasing complexity throughout the series. Practical topics in the lower levels progress to topics of interest and concern to more advanced students.

The *Canadian Concepts* Series is communicative in approach. The method offers productive strategies for language learning based on student-centred interaction. The pedagogical model presents students with challenging input, and provides activities that involve the students in information exchange. Students are often asked to work in pairs or groups to extend their understanding through interaction. Fluency activities are supported with spelling, dictation, pronunciation and writing tasks that focus on accuracy.

Canadian Concepts 2

Canadian Concepts 2 is a step up from beginners' level. Students build on skills through reviewing and expanding on themes from *Canadian Concepts 1*.

Students gain the confidence to function in English from the survival topics and cultural information, and are motivated to use their new skills in the real world through the Community Contact Tasks.

Teachers and students will appreciate the simplicity of the materials. Clear illustrations provide visual support and stimulate student discussion. Worksheets for some activities are provided in a special section of the Teacher's Manual, with permission to photocopy.

The Units

Canadian Concepts 2 is divided into 15 self-contained units. The units focus on survival topics and themes that are relevant to the students.

Each unit begins with an overview of topics and activities. The unit is then made up of a variety of activities that follow a basic three-part pattern. The first section introduces the subject. The next section calls for students to work with challenging material in the core reading or listening activity. Then the language is reviewed in a variety of ways.

The Activities

The "Get Ready" section provides reading or listening preparation. These pre-activities introduce the topic and generate interest in a variety of ways: through prediction exercises, discussion questions, dictation or interaction based on illustrations.

Core activities focus on taped passages or reading texts. They promote strategies of guessing from context, trying out possible answers and revising understanding through successive steps. Core activities consist of a variety of tasks: reading or listening for general information, reading or listening for detailed information, and listening for sounds.

Follow-up activities recycle language in the unit, providing an opportunity for students to express themselves and use new vocabulary. They include discussion activities, opportunities to practise language, vocabulary review, grammar review and writing.

Pre-Activities	Core Activities	Review and Recycle	Real-Life Application
Get Ready to Read	Read for General Ideas	Review Vocabulary	What About You?
Get Ready to Listen	Read for Details	Review Expressions	Tell the Story
Get Ready to Discuss	Read to Increase Speed	Practise Speaking	Express Yourself
	Listen for Meaning	Practise Grammar	Community Contact Tasks
	Listen for Details	Practise Writing	
	Listen for Sounds	Practise Numbers	
		Transfer Information	
		Exchange Information	
		Use Information	
		Dictations	
		Crossword Puzzles	
		Role Play	

Key to Symbols

| ⊙⊙ Listening Activity | □□ Work with a Partner |

☐ Reading Activity — □□/□□ Work in a Group

✎ Writing Activity — 😀😞 Role Play

Listening Programme

The listening programme in *Canadian Concepts 2* consists of survival English dialogues and short listening passages. Students listen to natural sounding Canadian English on topics relevant to their daily lives and activities. They are able to move through stages of comprehension as they listen first for general meaning, then for details and finally for sounds in reduced speech.

Teachers will appreciate that passages are recorded two or three times in sequence to avoid having to rewind and hunt for material on the tape during class.

Complete listening scripts and answer keys are provided with the Teacher's Manual. Listening worksheets are included in the Teacher's Manual.

Supplementary Grammar

Explanations of grammar points and practice exercises are provided in the Supplementary Grammar section. These exercises also review vocabulary from the preceding units. Suggestions for introducing grammar points are given in the Teacher's Manual.

Community Contact Tasks

The Community Contact Tasks are designed to complement activities done in class. They are linked to units in the book. Students have an opportunity to practise their English in real-life situations outside the classroom. A variety of tasks has been provided so that a selection can be made according to the needs and interests of the students in a particular class. Worksheets are provided in the Teacher's Manual.

Teacher's Manual

Each book in the series has its own Teacher's Manual that includes:

- step-by-step instructions keyed to the student's book;
- suggestions for classroom interaction;
- answers for exercises;

– tape scripts for listening activities;

– teacher's scripts for dictations and pronunciation exercises;

– student worksheets.

Detailed teacher's notes are included to make the intention of activities clear and to guide new teachers. Experienced teachers will find that the material lends itself to flexibility and accommodates individual teaching styles.

The authors wish success to their colleagues and the students who use these Canadian materials.

Lynda Berish
Sandra Thibaudeau

Acknowledgements

We would like to acknowledge the support and assistance of the following people in the classroom testing of the materials in this book: Maria De Rosa Wilson, Shelly Coleman, Dennis Plosker, Maryse Dodard and Terrance Clark. Their valuable comments, support and suggestions have been much appreciated.

We would like to thank friends and family who have supported our efforts: our patient husbands, John Berish and Charles Gruss, and our hungry children, Tara and Andrea Berish and Jean Baptiste, Gabrielle and Annabel Thibaudeau. We would like to thank Tara Berish and Jessica Dressler for their proofreading. We would also like to thank Howard Berish, Richard Goldman and Stephen Goldman for their advice, and Max and Millicent Goldman who, over many years and in many ways, have offered the kind of encouragement writers need to keep going.

We would like to express our sincere thanks to Elizabeth Taborek, from the Toronto Board, Continuing Education, Elisabeth Nadeau, Co-ordinator of ESL, Dorset Community College, Edna Downey and the instructors of CEGEP St. Jerome, Joan White of TESL Ottawa and Chris Cavan, Ottawa Board of Education, for their enthusiastic responses to our materials.

We would also like to express appreciation to our reviewers, Carole Trépanier (English Language Institute, University of British Columbia), Audrey Bonham (Community College Extension Centre, Red River College) and Marian Hislop (Palmer Junior Secondary School) for their encouraging comments and suggestions.

We would like to express appreciation to several people who have offered particular encouragement in the *Canadian Concepts* project: Yolanda de Rooy, Jerry Smith, Joe March, Kedre Murray, Marjorie Munroe, Linda Gorman and Karen Sacks. We would also like to express thanks for the technical expertise provided by Morris Apelbaum and Joe Chin, and for the invaluable editorial assistance of Elynor Kagan.

Our thanks go also to our families for the patience and help they have extended: to our husbands, John Berish and Charles Gruss, and to our children, Tara and Andrew Berish and Jean-Baptiste, Gabrielle and Annabel Thibaudeau. Thanks also to Howard Berish for his advice and assistance, and to Max and Millicent Goldman who, over many years and in many ways, have offered the kind of encouragement writers need to keep going.

The World

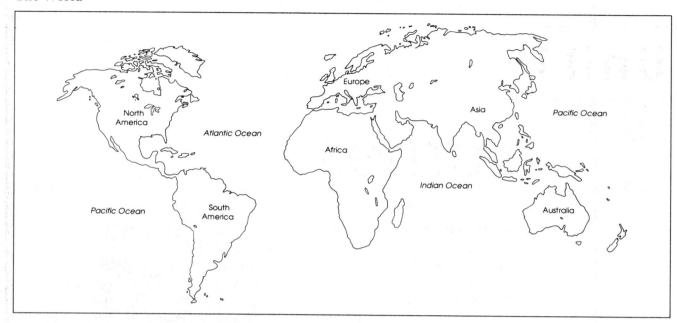

Europe

North
America

Atlantic Ocean

Asia

Pacific Ocean

Africa

Pacific Ocean

South
America

Indian Ocean

Australia

Canada

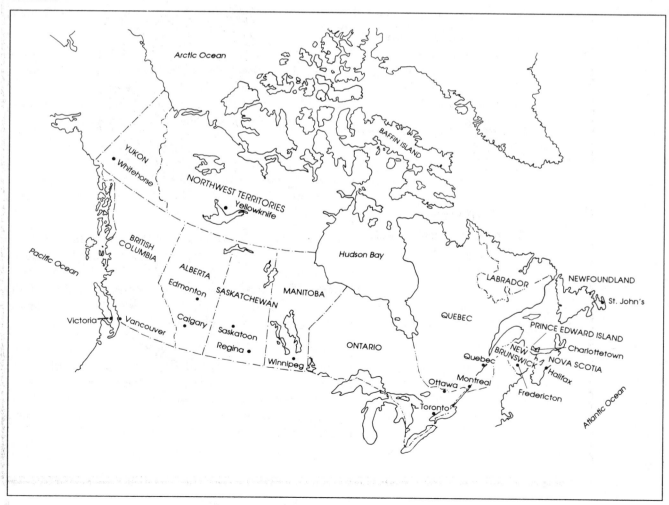

Arctic Ocean

BAFFIN ISLAND

YUKON

• Whitehorse

NORTHWEST TERRITORIES

• Yellowknife

BRITISH
COLUMBIA

Pacific Ocean

Hudson Bay

LABRADOR

NEWFOUNDLAND

ALBERTA

SASKATCHEWAN

MANITOBA

• St. John's

Edmonton •

QUEBEC

Victoria

• Vancouver

Calgary •

Saskatoon •

PRINCE EDWARD ISLAND

Regina •

ONTARIO

Charlottetown

Winnipeg •

Quebec •

NEW
BRUNSWICK

NOVA SCOTIA

Ottawa •

Montreal •

Halifax •

Fredericton •

Toronto •

Atlantic Ocean

Unit 1

Names

What Is Your Name?
Spelling
Interaction

Your Signature
Interaction

Names in the Class
Interaction

Names, Names, Names
Interaction

What About You?
Discussion

Different Places, Different Customs
Interaction
Reading

Personal Details: An Information Sheet
Writing

What Is Your Name?

Exercise 1: Get Ready

As your teacher spells out some common family names in Canada, write them down.

Exercise 2: Exchange Information

Ask three students the question, "What is your name?" Listen to them spell their names. Write the names down. Check the spelling carefully.

Your Signature

Exercise 1: Get Ready

When you write your name in block letters, like this: *John Bart* , it is called printing. When you write your name with the letters attached, like this: *John Bart* , it is called your signature.

Print your name, then sign your name.

Exercise 2: Exchange Information

Ask three people in your class to sign their names.

Names in the Class

On the board, write the name of another person in your class. Be sure to spell it correctly.

Names, Names, Names

Surnames

Most people have more than one name. Your last name is sometimes called your **surname** or **family name**. In the name **John Paul Bart**, Bart is the **surname**.

Write your surname.

Middle Names

Do you have a middle name? Some people have one or two names. Some people have three names. The name between the first name and the surname is the middle name.

What is the middle name?   John Paul Bart

Initials

 Initials are the first letters of each of your names.

1. Write the initials for John Paul Bart.

2. Write your initials.

3. Make a chart similar to the one below. Write the initials of three people in your group. Then write their full names.

	Initials	Name
Student A		
Student B		
Student C		

Nicknames

Nicknames are special forms of first names. Your family or good friends call you by your nickname. Match nicknames with first names:

Dick, Rick	William
Sandy	John
Jimmy (Jim)	Margaret
Johnny (Jack)	Thomas
Jackie	Edward
Tommy (Tom)	James
Teddy (Ted) Eddie (Ed)	Jacqueline
Mike (Mickey)	Elizabeth
Maggie (Margie)	Michael
Charlie (Chuck)	Robert
Liz, Beth	Catherine
Sue	Richard
Billy (Bill)	Sandra
Bob (Bobby)	Susan
Cathy	Charles

What About You?

Discuss these questions in a group.

1. What is your first name?

2. What do your friends call you?

3. Do you have a nickname?

4. What is your family name?

5. What is the formal way to address you: Mr., Miss, Ms., Mrs. or Dr.?

6. Does your name have a meaning? If it does, explain the meaning to your group.

Different Places, Different Customs

Exercise 1: Get Ready to Read

1. What are some popular names in your language? Make a list of four girls' names and four boys' names.

2. Check your lists in a group. How many names are the same?

Exercise 2: Read Quickly for General Ideas

Different Places, Different Customs

In most western European countries, people use their family names last, and begin with their given names. In countries such as England, Italy, France and Sweden, you find names such as Paul Lebrun and Maria Franco.

In China and Vietnam, family names come first and given names follow. Names look like this: Chao Jie or Ngugyen Nga. In Indonesia, many people don't use family names at all. They only have one name, like Subaryno or Hamdiyah.

In Canada most people have two or three names. They have a given name and surname, and sometimes a middle name. Parents give their children their first names and their middle names. Sometimes they give their children the same first name as another person in the family, for example, a grandparent or an aunt or uncle. Sometimes the parents just choose names they like for their children.

Exercise 3: Read Carefully for Details

Work with a partner. Look in the text for the answers.

1. What is the order for names in western Europe?

2. Give two examples of western European names from the text.

3. In China and Vietnam, which name comes first?

4. In Indonesia, how many names do most people have?

5. In Canada, how many names do most people have?

6. Who gives children their first and middle names?

7. Sometimes people get their names from people in the family. Give two examples.

8. What is another way that parents choose names for children?

Did You Know?	Some of the tallest people in the world live in Rwanda, Africa. Some people there are more than 210 centimetres tall. Some of the smallest people in the world also live in Africa. They live in Zaire. Many of them are only about 150 centimetres tall.

Personal Details: An Information Sheet

You use personal information to fill out application forms. Write personal details about you.

- Title (Mr., Miss, Ms., Mrs. or Dr.)
- First name, middle initials (if any) and last name
- Full address
- Telephone numbers at home and at work (including area code)
- Date of birth
- Marital status
- Spouse's name
- Name and relationship of next of kin

Unit 2

Telephones

The Telephone
Reading
Writing

Telephone Numbers
Number Dictation
Interaction

Change the Appointment
Listening Activity 1

Telephone Conversations
Dictation
Cultural Information

Can I Take a Message?
Listening Activity 2

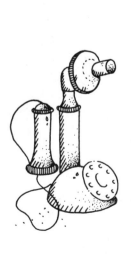

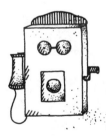

The Telephone

Exercise 1: Get Ready to Read

Discuss these questions in a group.

1. Do you know who invented the telephone?
2. In Canada, where do you get a telephone?
3. How much does it cost to use a public telephone in Canada?
4. How much does it cost to use a public telephone in other places? Give examples.

Exercise 2: Read Quickly for General Ideas

The Telephone

The telephone is the invention of a man named Alexander Graham Bell. It was invented in Nova Scotia, Canada. The first telephones were made of wood. People turned a handle to call the operator. The operator helped people to make telephone calls.

Later, telephones had dials. People began to dial the number that they wanted without the operator. The person who wanted to phone picked up the receiver and dialled a number. The other person heard the phone ring and picked up the receiver of his or her phone. Then the two people talked.

Today, people phone from their homes, offices and cars. Soon telephones will let you see the person you phone. Telephones will come with small televisions. What will people invent next?

Exercise 3: Read Carefully for Details

Read the text again. Then work with a partner to put these sentences in the same order as in the text.

1. People can phone from their cars.
2. People began to dial the number without the operator.
3. Telephones will let you see the person you phone.
4. The operator helped people make telephone calls.
5. Alexander Graham Bell invented the telephone.

Exercise 4: Practise Writing

Use the sentences to write a paragraph about the telephone.

Telephone Numbers

In North America, telephone numbers have seven numbers, which are called digits. We say them as single numbers.

Example: 739 4286

Exercise 1: Practise Numbers

Write the numbers that your teacher says.

Exercise 2: Exchange Information

Exchange telephone numbers with people in your group. Then discuss what you say when you phone someone. Examples include:

May I please speak to ____?

Is ____ there please?

Did You Know?   Telephones are important in an emergency. Look in your telephone book to find out which numbers to call in an emergency.

Change the Appointment

Listening Activity 1

Exercise 1: Get Ready to Listen

Caller　　　Receptionist

Before you begin, cover Exercise 4 on page 11.

Read these questions aloud with a partner. What do you think the conversation will be about?

1. The man's name is:
   a) Parker
   b) Barker
   c) Packer

2. The woman is:
   a) a doctor
   b) a receptionist
   c) a nurse

3. The appointment changes to another:
   a) place
   b) time
   c) day

4. The man says that:
   a) it's a problem
   b) it's OK
   c) it's too late

◯◯ Exercise 2: Listen for Meaning

Listen to the conversation. What is the conversation about?

◯◯ Exercise 3: Listen for Details

Go back to the questions. While you listen, choose the correct answers.

◯◯ Exercise 4: Listen for Sounds

While you listen, write the missing words.

Change the Appointment

Man:	Hello.
Receptionist:	Good morning, Mr. Barker?
Man:	No, ____ Mr. Packer. P-A-C-K-E-R.
Receptionist:	Excuse me. I didn't look carefully. _____ Dr. Chen's receptionist. Your appointment with the doctor ____ for Monday at 9:15.
Man:	Yes, 9:15, Monday. That's next week.
Receptionist:	The doctor wants ____ change the time. Can you come at 10:00 on Monday?
Man:	10:00, Monday? Sure. No problem. Thanks ____ calling. Goodbye.
Receptionist:	Goodbye Mr. Barker.

Exercise 5: Practise Speaking

☐☐ Practise reading the dialogue with a partner. Then change roles and read it again.

Telephone Conversations

Canadians talk on the phone a lot. They talk on the phone at work. They talk on the phone to their friends and families in the evenings. When it is cold outside, it is nice to stay home and talk on the phone.

Can I Take a Message?

Listening Activity 2

Exercise 1: Get Ready to Listen

Before you begin, cover Exercise 4 on page 13.

☐ ☐   Read the questions aloud with a partner. What do you think this conversation will be about?

1. Mr. Green is:
    a) at lunch
    b) out of the office
    c) in a meeting

2. The name of the caller is:
    a) W-E-A
    b) W-A-Y
    c) W-E-I

3. The time of the meeting must be changed because:
    a) someone is delayed
    b) someone is sick
    c) someone is on a trip

4. The new meeting time is:
    a) 10:30
    b) 2:30
    c) 4:30

5. The man promises to:
    a) give Mrs. Wei a message
    b) give Mr. Green a message
    c) change the meeting time

⊙ ⊙   ## Exercise 2: Listen for Meaning

Listen to the conversation. What is the conversation about?

○ ○   ## Exercise 3: Listen for Details

Go back to the questions. While you listen, choose the correct answers.

○ ○   ## Exercise 4: Listen for Sounds

While you listen, write the missing words.

Can I Take a Message?

Receptionist: Good morning, Alcan Aluminum.

Woman: Hello. _____ Mr. Green there please?

Receptionist: Sorry. _____ in a meeting. Can I take a message?

Woman: Yes. I'm Mrs. Wei.

Receptionist: Is that _ _ _ ?

Woman: No. It's _ _ _ .

Receptionist: OK. _ _ _ . And the message?

Woman: We have a meeting _____ 10:30 on Wednesday. Please tell him that Mr. Srolovitz can't be there before Wednesday afternoon. We have to change the meeting to 2:30, Thursday.

Receptionist: _____ sorry. How do you spell that?

Woman: T-H-U-R . . .

Receptionist: Excuse me. I _____ spell Thursday. How do you spell the man's name?

Woman: Oh, ha ha ha. Of course. S _ _ L _ _ _ T _ .

Receptionist: OK. I'll give him the message.

Woman: Thank you. Goodbye.

Receptionist: Goodbye.

Exercise 5: Practise Speaking

☐ ☐   Practise reading the dialogue with a partner. Then change roles and read it again.

Moving In

Finding a Place to Live
Reading
Interaction

Where I Live
Interaction

Finding a Place to Live

Exercise 1: Get Ready to Read

☐☐ In different cities in Canada, different words are used in the apartment ads in newspapers. Here are some abbreviations from ads for apartments in Vancouver. What do you think they mean?

Work with a partner to match each abbreviation to a word.

transp	immediate
prkg	bedrooms
lge	large
nr	parking
blk	basement
flr	building
bsmt	transportation
immed	floor
inc	included
bldg	block
bdrm	near

Exercise 2: Read Carefully for Information

These people are looking for places to live. Look at the ads. Then read about the people. Find apartments for each group of people. You can find more than one for each.

1. Available Immed. Lge. 3 bdrm. Quiet area. Bsmt. Near shops, schools, transit. Family welcome. Pets OK.

2. Luxury. Centrally located bldg. 2 bdrm. Beautiful view of city. Indoor pool.

3. Nice & clean 1 bdrm, nr schools, transit. Immed. Reasonable.

4. Modern clean. New hi-rise, 1 bdrm, inc. heat, hot water, prkg. No pets.

5. 2 bdrm centrally located, pets OK, very clean, near shops, transport, across from park.

6. Free 1/2 Month Rent! 1 bdrm, available immed, close to everything.

7. Clean & quiet. Bright 3 bdrm, quiet area, central, immed, bsmt, 2 flr, 1 blk from transp, school, new carpets.

Finding a Place to Live

Alvaro and Mauricio are students. They come from Mexico. They study English in Canada. They want to share an apartment. They want to find a small apartment that is close to class. Their school is downtown. They both have part-time jobs, but they do not have a lot of money to spend.

Mr. and Mrs. Lin are looking for a house to rent. Mr. Lin works in an insurance agency. Mrs. Lin works at a bank. Mr. and Mrs. Lin have two small children. They would like a house that has a back yard so the children can play outside. They want to be close to a school. They have lots of furniture and toys. They also have a dog and a cat.

Shirley and Henry are getting married. Shirley is a lawyer. Henry has his own business. They have enough money to afford a nice apartment. They want an apartment that has a good view of the city. They also need a garage for their car.

Mrs. James is a single mother. She has a four-year-old son. She works as a nurse in a large hospital. Her son goes to day care every day. She wants to find a small apartment that is close to her work and to the day care. She needs to be close to public transportation.

Where I Live

Exercise 1: Get Ready

Draw a floor plan of where you live (your house or your apartment).

Exercise 2: Exchange Information

Exchange drawings with a partner. Tell your partner three things that are in each room. Ask your partner to write the names of these things on **your** drawing.

Unit 4

In the House

Around the House
Vocabulary

Where's the Milk?
Listening Activity 3

Living Together
Reading

A. Jessica is Neat
Reading
Interaction

B. Tara is Messy
Reading
Interaction
A and B: Information Exchange

Prepositions of Place
Grammar

Tara's Room
Vocabulary

The Lost Shoe
Listening Activity 4

Choices
Dictation

What About You?
Discussion

At Home
Crossword Puzzle

Around the House

Exercise 1: Get Ready

Work with a partner. Look at the pictures of things in the house. How many can you name?

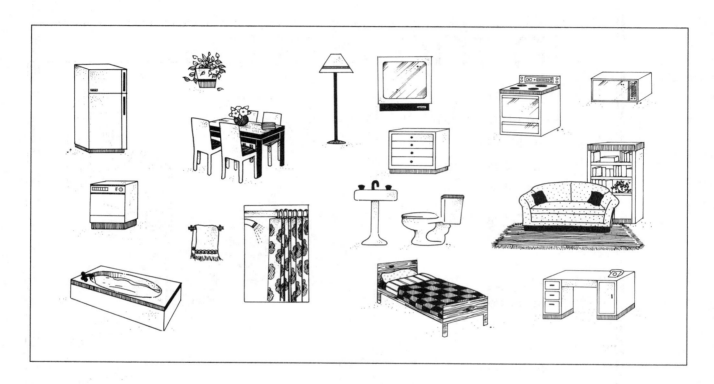

Exercise 2: Use Information

Make a chart similar to the one below. Put each object in the correct room. Some objects will go in more than one room.

Kitchen	Bedroom	Living Room	Bathroom

bed   table   couch   bathtub   refrigerator   plant   lamp   dishes
television set   stove   chairs   dishwasher   desk   sink   bureau
carpet   toilet   shower   microwave   curtains   bookcase   towels

Where's the Milk?

Listening Activity 3

Exercise 1: Get Ready to Listen

☐☐ **A.** Look at these pictures. Work with a partner to find the objects from the list.

fridge

milk

orange juice

flowers

flower vase

eggs

goldfish bowl

cookie jar

pot

egg carton

☐☐ **B.** Read these questions aloud with a partner. What do you think the conversation will be about?

1. The milk is in the orange juice container. **T** (true) or **F** (false)?

2. The orange juice is in the _____ vase.

3. The flowers are in the _____ jar.

4. Tara ate some flowers. **T F**

5. The _____ are in the goldfish bowl.

6. The goldfish are in the _____.

7. Jessica wants to drink _____.

8. What is in the pot?

When you turn to page 20, cover Exercise 4.

○ ○ **Exercise 2: Listen for Meaning**

Jessica wants some milk. Listen to the conversation. What is the conversation about?

○ ○ **Exercise 3: Listen for Details**

Go back to the questions. While you listen, answer the questions.

○ ○ **Exercise 4: Listen for Sounds**

While you listen, write the missing words.

Where's the Milk?

Jessica: Tara, where'_____ the milk?

Tara: It's in the fridge, Jessica.

Jessica: Where _____ the fridge?

Tara: Oh, the milk carton tore. I put the milk in _____ orange juice container.

Jessica: Where _____ you put the orange juice, Tara?

Tara: I put the orange juice in _____ flower vase.

Jessica: Where did you put the flowers?

Tara: _____ put the flowers in the cookie jar.

Jessica: Where did you put the cookies?

Tara: Well, I ate some _____ the cookies. I put the rest in the egg carton.

Jessica: Where did you put the eggs?

Tara: I put the eggs_____ the goldfish bowl.

Jessica: In the goldfish bowl? Where are the goldfish?

Tara: Oh, I put the goldfish _____ the pot.

Jessica: But I want some hot milk.

Tara: So use the pot, Jessica.

Jessica: I _____ use the pot, Tara! The fish are in _____ !

Exercise 5: Practise Speaking

□ □ Practise reading the dialogue with a partner. Then change roles and read it again.

Living Together

Exercise 1: Get Ready to Read

☐ ☐ Look at the pictures of Tara and Jessica. They have a problem. What do you think it is?

Exercise 2: Read Quickly for General Ideas

Living Together

Tara and Jessica are roommates. They live in an apartment together. They are both students who study English.

Tara and Jessica like to live together. But they have one problem — a big problem. Jessica is very neat. Tara is very messy. Sometimes when Jessica comes home from class, she finds a big mess in the apartment. She gets very angry at Tara.

Exercise 3: Read Carefully for Details

Work with a partner. Look in the text for the answers.

1. Where do Tara and Jessica live?

2. What do they study?

3. What is their problem?

4. Why does Jessica get angry at Tara?

Exercise 4: Review Vocabulary

Match the opposites:

good	remember
messy	never
clean	find
always	bad
big	neat
forget	dirty
early	small
lose	late

Jessica is Neat

Partner A

Exercise 1: Get Ready to Read

☐☐ Look at the pictures of Jessica. What is she doing?

Exercise 2: Read Quickly for General Ideas

Jessica is Neat

Jessica is very neat in the apartment. Every morning Jessica makes her bed, and cleans up her room. After breakfast, she puts the leftover food in the refrigerator and washes the dishes. Then she dries the dishes and puts them away in the cupboard.

When she comes home from class, she hangs her clothes in the closet. She does her homework, and then puts her books in her bag.

Exercise 3: Read Carefully for Details

Work with a partner. Look in the text for the answers.

1.   What does Jessica do when she wakes up?

2.   After breakfast, she leaves the food on the table. True or false?

3.   Where does she put the dishes?

4.   What does Jessica do when she comes home from class?

5.   Where does she put her books?

Exercise 4: Transfer Information

Make a chart similar to the one below.

What Jessica does every day		What Tara does every day	
In the morning	After class	In the morning	After class

Write the information about Jessica on the chart.

Exercise 5: Exchange Information

Ask your partner for information about Tara. Write the information on your chart.

Did You Know?   Winters are cold in Canada, but Canadians know how to keep warm. Homes in Canada are well heated. The walls, doors and windows of Canadian buildings keep the heat inside.

Tara is Messy

Partner B

Exercise 1: Get Ready to Read

☐ ☐ Look at the pictures. What do you see in the bedroom? What do you see in the kitchen?

Exercise 2: Read Quickly for General Ideas

Tara is Messy

In the morning when Tara has breakfast, she leaves things everywhere. She leaves the milk on the counter. She cooks an egg, and forgets to eat it. She leaves dirty dishes on the table. She leaves crumbs on the floor.

Tara's room is a huge mess. When she comes home, she throws her jacket on the floor. Then she drops her books beside her jacket. She takes off her sneakers and kicks them under the bed. On top of her jacket, she throws the newspaper and maybe some magazines.

Exercise 3: Read Carefully for Details

Work with a partner. Look in the text for the answers .

1. Where does Tara leave the milk?
2. Where does Tara leave her dishes?
3. Where does Tara put her jacket?
4. Where does Tara put her shoes?
5. What does Tara put on top of her jacket?

Exercise 4: Transfer Information

Make a chart similar to the one below. Write the information about Tara in your chart.

What Jessica does every day		What Tara does every day	
In the morning	After class	In the morning	After class

Exercise 5: Exchange Information

Ask your partner for information about Jessica. Write the information on your chart.

Did You Know?	Most houses or apartments in Canada have one or more bedrooms, a living room, a kitchen and a bathroom. Bigger homes have more bedrooms or bathrooms and extra rooms, such as a dining room or a den.

Prepositions of Place

Exercise 1: Get Ready

☐☐ Work with a partner. Look at the picture of the living room. How many objects can you name?

**bookcase   couch   picture   basket   dog   lamp   table   plant
calendar   cup   glass   glasses   wall   floor   carpet**

Exercise 2: Use Prepositions

☐☐ Look at the picture and choose the correct preposition for each sentence.

in   on   over   under   near   between   beside

1. The picture is _____ the couch.
2. The lamp is _____ the couch.
3. The dog is _____ the basket.
4. The girl is _____ the couch.
5. The couch is _____ the bookcase.
6. The carpet is _____ the chair.
7. The books are _____ the bookcase.

8. The calendar is _____ the wall.

9. The carpet is _____ the floor.

10. The glasses are _____ the table.

11. The glass is _____ the glasses.

12. The couch is _____ the lamp and the bookcase.

Exercise 3: Practise Writing

Write six sentences about the location of objects in the living room.

Tara's Room

Look at the picture of Tara's room. Choose the correct word for each space.

lamp   jacket   floor   bed   dog   bureau   guitar

Tara's room is a big mess. Her sheets and blankets are on the _____. Her sweater
                                                              1

is under her _____. Her socks are on the _____. Her pillow is on her _____. Her
            2   **3**   **4**

books are under her _____. Her _____ is on her bed. Her scarf is on her _____.
                   5   **6**   **7**

The Lost Shoe

Listening Activity 4

Exercise 1: Get Ready to Listen

Before you begin, cover Exercise 4 on page 29.

☐☐ **A.** Look at the pictures. Work with a partner to answer the questions.

Tara has lost something. What did she lose? Where did she look? Did she find it? What is the problem now?

☐☐ **B.** Read these questions aloud with a partner. What do you think the conversation will be about?

1. Tara lost her hat.   **T** (true) or **F** (false)?

2. Tara has her left shoe.   **T   F**

3. The left shoe was in the kitchen.   **T   F**

4. The right shoe was under the couch.   **T   F**

5. The right shoe was in the kitchen.   **T   F**

6. The right shoe was in the cupboard.   **T   F**

7. Tara is ready to go to class.   **T   F**

8. What was missing?

Exercise 2: Listen for Meaning

Listen to the conversation. What is the conversation about?

Exercise 3: Listen for Details

Go back to the questions. While you listen, write **T** (true) or **F** (false).

Exercise 4: Listen for Sounds

While you listen, write the missing words.

The Lost Shoe

Tara: I ____ find my shoe. My running shoe. The white one. Did you see it?

Jessica: You lost your shoe, Tara?

Tara: Well, I didn't really lose my shoe. I just can't find ____. I have my left shoe. I can't find my right shoe.

Jessica: Where was the left shoe?

Tara: The left shoe was in the living room. It was near the couch.

Jessica: Did ____ look behind the couch?

Tara: Yes, I looked everywhere. I looked under the couch. I looked on ____ couch. I looked behind the couch.

Jessica: And?

Tara: And? And the shoe wasn't there.

Jessica: How about in the kitchen? Maybe your shoe is in the kitchen.

Tara: I looked in the kitchen. I looked under the table. I looked in ____ cupboard. I looked behind the curtains. I even looked under the sink. My shoe wasn't there.

Jessica: Hmmmm. How about in the bedroom? Did you look in the bedroom?

Tara: Good idea. I'____ go look there now.

Jessica: OK. But hurry. We'll be late ____ class.

Tara: Guess what? I found my shoe! First I looked on the bed. Then I looked under the bed. Then I looked on my dresser. Then I looked in all my drawers. And finally I found it. ____ was in the cupboard, under my sweater.

Jessica: Tara, that's great. Are you ready ____ leave for class now?

Tara: Well, not yet.

Jessica: What do you mean, not yet? What's wrong now?

Tara: I ____ find my right sock!

Exercise 5: Practise Speaking

☐ ☐   Practise reading the dialogue with a partner. Then change roles and read it again.

Exercise 6: Tell the Story

☐ ☐   Tell the story of the lost sock to your partner. Use the pictures to help you. Then your partner will tell you the story.

Choices

People live in different places. Some people live in houses. Other people live in apartments. Some people live with their families. Some people live with roommates. Some people live alone. Some people have a dog or a cat for a pet.

What About You?

☐☐
☐☐   Discuss these questions in a group

1. Do you live alone or with someone else?

2. Do you like to live with another person? Why?

3. Do you have any problems with the person or people you live with? What are the problems?

4. Are you neat or messy?

5. Is the person that you live with neat or messy?

At Home

Crossword Puzzle

Across

3. I eat at the _____.
5. I cook food in the _____.
7. I keep my food cold in the _____.
8. I sleep in the _____.
10. I sit on the _____ in the living room.
12. I take a bath in the _____.
13. I do my homework at my _____.

Down

1. I cook food on the _____.
2. I wash dishes in the _____.
4. My couch is in the _____.
6. I sit on a _____.
9. After I eat, I wash my _____.
11. I live in a _____.

Families

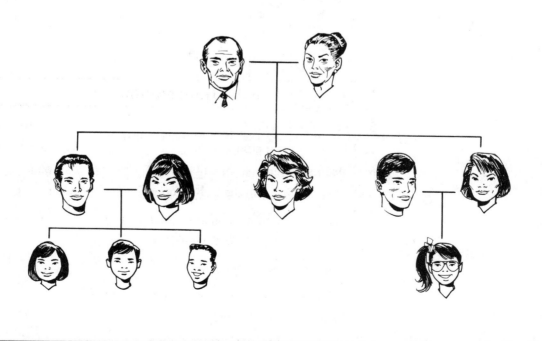

Metropolitan Separate School Board
Continuing Education Dept.
ADULT ENGLISH CLASSES

33

The Family Tree

Exercise 1: Get Ready

☐☐ Look at the family tree. Work with a partner to identify the following people:

grandparents   parents   children

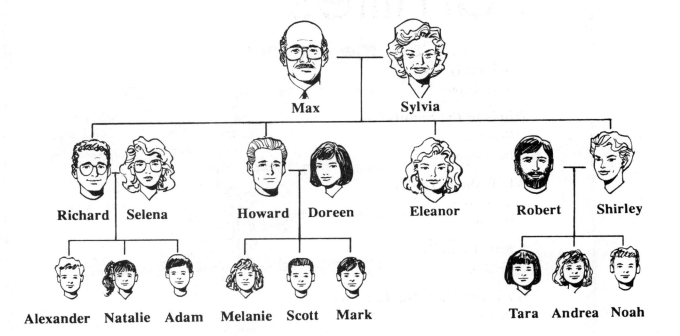

Exercise 2: Use the Information

☐☐ Work with a partner to answer these questions.

1. Who are Andrea's parents?

2. Who are Andrea's grandparents?

3. Who are Andrea's cousins? (Name six.)

4. Who is Richard's wife?

5. Who is Doreen's husband?

6. Who are Sylvia's daughters? (Name two.)

7. Who is Shirley's son?

8. Who is Alexander's sister?

9. Who are Melanie's aunts? (Name four.)

10. Who are Eleanor's nephews? (Name five.)

11. Who is Mark's brother?

12. Who are Noah's uncles? (Name two.)

13. Who are Max's granddaughters? (Name four.)

14. Who is Howard's wife?

15. Who are Melanie's brothers? (Name two.)

Who's in the Family?

Exercise 1: Get Ready to Read

Look at the family tree. Work with a partner to answer these questions.

1. How many people are in the family?

2. How many adults are in the family?

3. How many children are in the family?

4. How many people are male?

5. How many people are female?

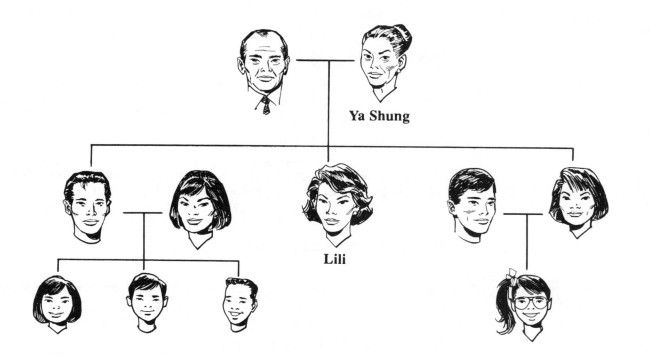

Exercise 2: Read Quickly for General Ideas

Who's in the Family?

Liu and Ya Shung are husband and wife. They married in 1931. They are parents. They have three children. They have a son and two daughters. Their son is named Yong. Their daughters are Lili and Jenny. Lili is single. Jenny is married.

Yong is married to Amy. Yong and his wife Amy have three children, Rose, Jie and Jack.

Lili is single. Her sister is Jenny. Her brother is Yong.

Jenny is married to Steve. Jenny and her husband have one daughter, Joyce. Joyce is the cousin of Rose, Jie and Jack.

Exercise 3: Read Carefully for Details

Read the text again. Then work with a partner to name the people on the family tree.

Exercise 4: Practise Writing

Write seven sentences to describe the relationships in the family.

> Example: Jenny is Yong's sister.

What About You?

Exercise 1: Get Ready

Make your own family tree. Draw and label:

**your grandparents   your parents   you   your sisters and brothers
your aunts and uncles   your cousins**

Exercise 2: Exchange Information

Show your family tree to students in your group. Tell them about your family.

Exercise 3: Practise Writing

Write about your family.

A Royal Family

Exercise 1: Get Ready to Read

Look at the stamp. Work with a partner to answer the questions.

1. Who is the woman on the stamp?
2. Why is she on the stamp?
3. What is another place that we see this woman's picture?

Reproduction courtesy of Canada Post Corporation

Exercise 2: Read Quickly for General Ideas

A Royal Family

The woman we see on stamps and money in Canada is Queen Elizabeth II. She is Queen of England and several other countries. She is Queen of Canada because Canada was once a colony of England. Elizabeth became queen in 1952. She was in Africa, on a royal tour with her husband, when she learned that her father was dead and she was queen.

Queen Elizabeth and her husband, Prince Phillip, have four children. Their daughter, Princess Anne, has two children. She loves horses. Their other three children are Charles, Andrew and Edward.

Charles, who is the oldest son, may be king one day. Like his sister Anne, Charles likes horses. He plays polo. Princess Diana is famous for her beauty and for her elegant clothes. Charles and Diana have two sons.

Andrew, who is the second oldest son, is an officer in the navy. He married Lady Sarah. She is famous for her red hair and her spirit of adventure. She flies a helicopter. Andrew and Sarah have two daughters.

Prince Edward is the youngest son. He is not married. He loves the theatre and he is a good actor. Sometimes he puts on plays for the royal family. He asks his nieces and nephews to be in the plays. He also asks his brothers and sister.

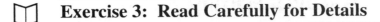

Exercise 3: Read Carefully for Details

Work with a partner. Look in the text for the answers.

1. When did Elizabeth become queen?

2. Where was she when her father died?

3. Name the Queen's children in order of age.

4. Give information about Princess Anne in note form.

5. Why will Charles be king one day?

6. Give information about Charles in note form.

7. Give two reasons why Princess Diana is famous.

8. What is Prince Andrew's job?

9. How many grandchildren do the Queen and Prince Phillip have?

10. What does Prince Edward like?

11. Who does he ask to be in his plays?

Small Families, Big Families

In western countries, many families are small. Parents have one or two children. In other parts of the world, families are sometimes very large. Parents, children and grandparents may all live in the same house. Sometimes aunts and uncles live in the house too.

Unit 6

Jobs

Who Does These Jobs?
Reading

Jobs, Jobs, Jobs
Interaction
Vocabulary
Writing

A Job You Like
Interaction
Writing

Getting Fired
Dictation

Who Does These Jobs?

Exercise 1: Get Ready to Read

Work with a partner. Look at the pictures of people doing different jobs. How many jobs can you name?

Exercise 2: Read Carefully for Information

Read the paragraphs. Then write the name of the job for each description.

nurse   plumber   hairdresser   photographer   firefighter   taxi driver
letter carrier   sales clerk   hockey player   police officer   pilot   actor

1. This person skates on the ice very fast. This person tries to win a game. The game is a sport that is famous in Canada. Many people like to watch this game. They yell and cheer. It is fun to watch the game.

2. This person walks a lot. When it is hot or cold outside, when it rains or snows, this person brings mail to people at their homes. This person delivers letters, magazines and packages.

3. This person helps you when you want to look different. When your hair is too long, or you don't like the style, this person washes your hair and cuts it. Then he or she dries your hair and makes it look nice.

4. This person helps you when you are sick in the hospital. This person helps the doctor. This person gives medicine, washes the sick people and helps the sick people eat.

5. This person drives a car all day. You call this person to take you somewhere when you are in a hurry and you don't have a car. You can call this person on the telephone. He or she will come to your house to get you. This person will take you where you want to go. You pay this person when you arrive.

6. When you go to a store to buy clothes, this person helps you. This person helps you find the right size and the right colour. When you buy clothes, you pay this person. Then he or she puts your clothes in a bag for you.

Exercise 3: Transfer Information

Make a chart similar to the one below. List the jobs you named. Then write three things that each person does.

	Job	Things the person does
1.		
2.		
3.		
4.		
5.		
6.		

Jobs, Jobs, Jobs

Exercise 1: Get Ready

☐ ☐   Discuss the list of jobs. Make a chart and put the jobs into categories.

office clerk	mechanic
lawyer	receptionist
engineer	electrician
secretary	manager
plumber	nurse
dentist	carpenter

Profession	Trade	Office Work

Exercise 2: Review Vocabulary

Match the information about jobs.

Example: a secretary   in an office   types letters

a waiter	in a hotel	sells shoes
a teller	in a hospital	types letters
a nurse	in a store	serves food
a sales clerk	in a bank	helps passengers
a secretary	in a plane	cashes cheques
a doorman	in a restaurant	opens doors
a stewardess	in an office	gives shots

Exercise 3: Practise Writing

Use the information to write sentences about people's jobs.

Example: He is a teller. He works in a bank. He cashes cheques.

Remember: The third person singular form of the verb ends with **s**.

A Job You Like

Exercise 1: Exchange Information

Interview three students. Find three jobs that people in their families do. Write the jobs on a chart similar to the one below.

	Student A	Student B	Student C
1.			
2.			
3.			

Exercise 2: Practise Writing

Write about a job you like or would like to do.

Getting Fired

In Taiwan, it is a custom for bosses to invite their employees to the house for dinner. The boss serves them chicken, but people are afraid to look at their plates. This is because, when the boss wants to fire an employee, the custom is to serve a chicken head.

City Life

Exercise 1: Get Ready to Read

☐ ☐   Work with a partner. Look at the picture of the city.

1. List three jobs that people do in the city.
2. List three kinds of entertainment.
3. List three places to buy things.
4. List two places to mail a letter.
5. List two kinds of public transportation.
6. Name a place to live.
7. Name a place to stay for a few days.
8. List two places to sit and relax.
9. List three ways to drive in the city.
10. Name a place to park a car.
11. List two places where cars have to stop.
12. List two things that help you cross the street.
13. Name something that tells you where you are.
14. List two things that grow in the city.
15. Name a place to get water if there is a fire.
16. List two places where you can get a book to read.

Exercise 2: Read Quickly for General Ideas

City Life

Do you live in the city or in the country? Many people live in the city. In cities there are jobs and there are places to live. People like to live in cities because there are a lot of services. For example, there are schools, hospitals, stores and transportation.

A city can be very exciting. There are many things to do in the city. For entertainment, you can go to a movie or to the theatre. You can go to a good restaurant, a concert or a ball game. Cities have parks where people go to see trees, flowers and small animals. At night, the city is full of coloured lights. It can look very beautiful.

The city can be crowded. There are cars, buses and taxicabs on the roads. Sometimes there are so many cars that all the traffic stops. This happens in the morning, when people go to work, or at night, when people come home from work. When there are too many cars on the road, it is faster to take a subway or even to walk.

Exercise 3: Read Carefully for Details

Work with a partner. Look in the text for the answers.

1. Name two things you can find in cities.
2. Name four services in cities.
3. Name five places you can go for entertainment.
4. Name three things you can see in the park.
5. Name something you can see at night in the city.
6. Name three kinds of transportation in the city.
7. Name two times of day when the traffic stops.
8. Name two ways you can travel when the traffic stops.

Exercise 4: Review Vocabulary

Find the word that does not belong in each line.

1. museum   egg   concert   movie   theatre
2. car   truck   bus   ice cream   taxicab
3. movie   snow   rain   sun   wind
4. mountain   ocean   river   table   forest
5. apartment   building   house   apple   office
6. walk   run   hurry   go   tree

City and Country

Listening Activity 5

Exercise 1: Get Ready to Listen

A.   Work in a group. Look at the pictures. First list some things you can do in the city. Then list some things you can do in the country. Try to add your own ideas as well.

Example:

In the city you can go to the movies.

In the country you can ride a horse.

☐☐ **B.** Read these questions aloud with a partner. What do you think this conversation will be about?

1. Carla likes the city.   **T** (true) or **F** (false)?
2. Ali likes to go to movies and concerts.   **T   F**
3. Carla thinks the city is noisy.   **T   F**
4. Carla likes to work in a big city.   **T   F**
5. Carla likes to walk in the country.   **T   F**
6. Ali and Carla want to visit each other.   **T   F**

When you turn to page 48, cover Exercise 4.

▣ Exercise 2: Listen for Meaning

Listen to the conversation. What is the conversation about?

▣ Exercise 3: Listen for Details

Go back to the questions. While you listen, write **T** (true) or **F** (false) for each question.

▣ Exercise 4: Listen for Sounds

While you listen, write the missing words.

City and Country

Ali: I come from the city. I come from a big city.

Carla: Ali, do you like _____ live in the city?

Ali: Yes, I do, Carla. There are lots _____ things to do in the city.

Carla: What can you do in the city?

Ali: In the city? Oh, you _____ go to the movies or a concert. You can go to the museum or a park. You can go to a ball game or you can eat in a good restaurant.

Carla: But the city is very noisy. There are so many people in the city. There are so many cars _____ the city.

Ali: That's true. But there are also lots of parks _____ go to.

Carla: I prefer the country.

Ali: Why? The country is so quiet. There's nothing _____ do in the country.

Carla: Oh yes, there are lots _____ things to do in the country. You can go for a long walk. You can have a picnic. You can listen to the birds sing. In the summer, you _____ swim in the lake.

Ali: Hmmm, that sounds pretty nice. Maybe I'_____ come visit you in the country some time.

Carla: Maybe I'll visit you in the city.

Exercise 5: Practise Speaking

☐☐ Practise reading the dialogue with a partner. Then change roles and read it again.

Museums

On a rainy day in the city, some people like to visit museums. Museums are interesting places. You can learn about things that happened long ago, see beautiful paintings or learn about life in other places.

Exercise 1: Get Ready to Read

A. Work in a group. Look at the pictures of different things you can find in museums. How many things can you name?

B. Make a chart similar to the one below. Write the objects from the museums in the chart.

History Museum	Art Museum	Science and Technology Museum	Aquarium

Exercise 2: Read for Information

Read the text. While you read, look for examples of things you can find in each museum. Add new information to your chart.

Museums

In the city, there are different kinds of museums. There are different things to see in each museum.

A history museum has things from the past. You can find out how people lived long ago. You can learn about the clothes and jewellery people wore, the kinds of dishes and furniture they had and the tools they used.

An art museum has paintings, sculpture and photographs from different parts of the world. You can learn about the past from paintings and sculptures. There are also paintings and sculptures that are not very old. They are called modern art.

In the science and technology museum you can see how things work. You can learn about machines and tools. From looking at old machines and tools, you can learn about how people lived in the past. You can also learn about plants and animals in different parts of the world.

An aquarium is a kind of museum for fish and animals that live in the water. You can see big fish, such as sharks, and smaller fish, such as angel fish. Sometimes you can see penguins, which are birds. You can also see the plants that grow in the ocean. If you like the ocean, an aquarium is a great place to go.

Exercise 3: Read Carefully for Details

Read the text again. Then work with a partner to answer the questions.

1. Write two ways to say **before**.
2. Name two kinds of museums where you can learn about the past.
3. Write the words that we use for paintings that are not old.
4. Name two things that give information about how people lived in the past.
5. Name three things that live in water.

What About You?

Exercise 1: Get Ready

Think about a city that you know. Answer the questions.

1. The city is:
   a) big
   b) small
   c) middle size

2. The city has:
   a) fewer than 1 million people
   b) between 1 and 3 million people
   c) more than 3 million people

3. The city is near:
   a) a mountain
   b) a river
   c) an ocean
   d) other

4. In winter, the city is:
   a) very cold
   b) cool
   c) warm
   d) rainy
   e) other

5. In summer, the city is:
   a) hot
   b) warm
   c) cool
   d) other

Did You Know?   The area around Tokyo, Japan is the most populated urban area in the world. It has more than 28 million people.

6. The city has:
   a) four seasons
   b) two seasons

7. In the city, people travel by:
   a) bus
   b) subway
   c) car
   d) train
   e) bicycle
   f) other

8. Some of the things you can find in the city are:
   a) movies
   b) theatres
   c) zoos
   d) parks
   e) concert halls
   f) museums
   g) sports stadiums
   h) department stores
   i) skyscrapers
   j) restaurants

Exercise 2: Exchange Information

In a group, talk about a city that you know. Use the information from the quiz to help you.

A City I Know

Write about a city that you know.

Where Do You Find It?

It is sometimes difficult to know where to buy things in a city or town. We all know that you can buy a chair in a furniture store. Did you know that you can also buy a chair in a hardware store? We all know that you can buy stamps at the post office. Do you know other places to buy stamps?

Look at the list of things you sometimes need to buy. Where do you think you can buy them? Make a chart similar to the one below and write the name of the articles under the store or stores where you can find them.

toothpaste   cookies   coffee   bread   aspirin   a hammer   mugs
a newspaper   a dictionary   a tea kettle   medicine   milk   writing paper
stamps   paint   a birthday cake

Hardware Store	Corner Store	Bakery

Bookstore	Supermarket	Drugstore

Neighbourhoods

Choose the correct word for each space.

foods   people   neighbourhoods   schools   city

Cities have many different areas, called ____ . Each neighbourhood has its own
1
____ , shopping areas, churches and sports arena. Each neighbourhood has its
2
own restaurants with special ____ . In a big ____ , you can't meet everyone. But
3   4
you can meet the ____ in your neighbourhood. They are your neighbours.
5

Buying a Tea Kettle

> **Listening Activity 6**

Exercise 1: Get Ready to Listen

Before you begin, cover Exercise 4 on page 55.

☐ ☐   Read the questions aloud with a partner. What do you think the conversation will
be about?

1. The men live:
    a) in the same apartment
    b) in the same building
    c) next door to each other

2. The man wants to buy:
    a) a new clock
    b) some tea
    c) a kettle

3. You can buy a kettle:
    a) at the shoe store
    b) at the hardware store
    c) at the bookstore

4. The man will also buy:
    a) a tea kettle
    b) a package of matches
    c) some light bulbs

5. The man thinks that buying light bulbs is:
   a) too much trouble
   b) too expensive
   c) no problem

Exercise 2: Listen for Meaning

Listen to the conversation. What is the conversation about?

Exercise 3: Listen for Details

Go back to the questions. While you listen, choose the correct answers.

Exercise 4: Listen for Sounds

While you listen, write the missing words.

Buying a Tea Kettle

George: Excuse me. I'____ George, your new neighbour. I live in the apartment across the hall.

Spiros: I know. You moved ____ yesterday. Nice to meet you. I'm Spiros. Can I help you with something?

George: Yes, please. I need a kettle to boil water ____ tea. Where can I buy one?

Spiros: Oh, you can buy a kettle _____ Eaton's or the Bay. But I think Johnson's Hardware is closer. It's just around the corner. Yes, why don't you try ____ hardware store.

George: It's just around the corner? Maybe that's the best place. Thanks. Thanks ____ lot.

Spiros: While ____ there, can you get a package of light bulbs for me?

George: Light bulbs? OK, sure. No problem. How much do they cost?

Spiros: I'____ not sure. Here's $2. I think it's enough.

George: OK. Thanks for your help. See ____ later.

Exercise 5: Practise Speaking

Practise reading the dialogue with a partner. Then change roles and read it again.

How Do I Get There?

Map A

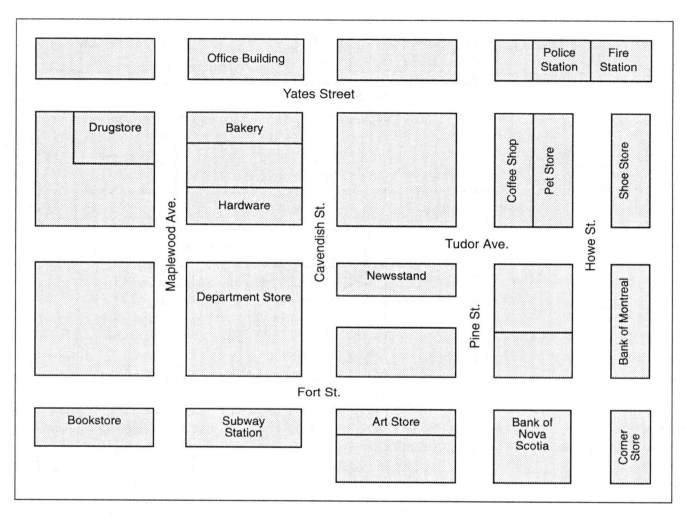

Partner A

Ask your partner these questions. Use the map to follow the directions your partner gives you. Find the places. Then answer your partner's questions.

1. I'm at the subway station. How do I get to the library?

2. I need to buy stamps. How do I get from the corner of Maplewood and Fort to the post office?

3. I'm at the library. How do I get to the supermarket?

4. I'm at the Bank of Montreal. How do I get to the restaurant?

5. I'm at the corner of Pine and Yates. How do I get to the gift shop?

Map B

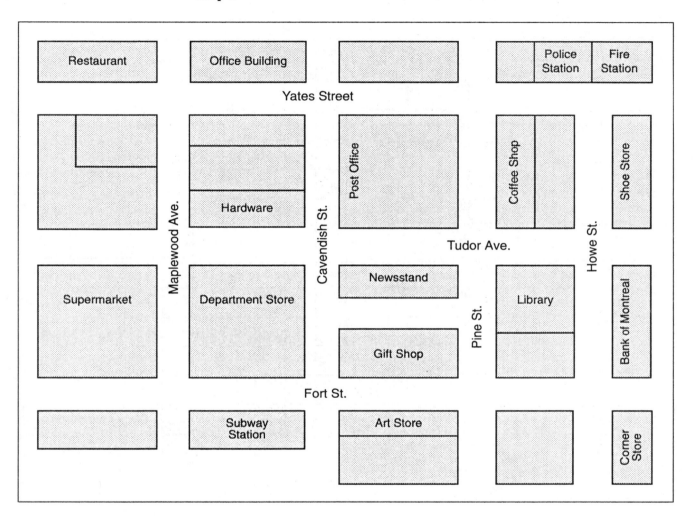

Partner B

☐☐ Use the map to answer your partner's questions. Then ask your partner these questions. Find the places. Follow the directions your partner gives you.

1. I'm at the subway station. How do I get to the drugstore?

2. I need a dictionary. How do I get from the corner of Pine and Tudor to the bookstore?

3. I'm at the library. I want to go to the bakery. How do I get there?

4. I'm at the shoe store. How do I get to the pet store?

5. I'm at the drugstore. How do I get to the Bank of Nova Scotia?

In the City

Crossword Puzzle

Across

2. I like to watch a good ____.

4. If you don't have a car, you can take a ____.

6. A ____ is a good way to travel in the city.

7. Go to the ____ when you need to buy something.

8. When the traffic light is ____ you can go.

11. At rush hour, there is a lot of ____ downtown.

12. Many ____ live in a city.

Down

1. I like to eat lunch in a ____.

2. You can learn about many new things in a ____.

3. I live in a big ____.

5. I see squirrels and birds in the ____ near my house.

7. A ____ is an animal that lives in the city.

9. When the traffic light is ____ you must stop.

10. To mail a letter, you can put the letter in the ____.

Unit 8

The Mail

Mail
Reading
Vocabulary
Grammar

How to Address an Envelope
Reading
Writing
Cultural Information

Provinces
Dictation

At the Post Office
Listening Activity 7

Mail

Exercise 1: Get Ready

Discuss these questions in a group.

1. How do you mail a letter in Canada?
2. What colour are mailboxes?
3. Where can you buy stamps?
4. Where do you receive mail?

Exercise 2: Read Quickly for General Ideas

Mail

Mailboxes are on street corners all over the city. In Canada, mailboxes are always red. The mail is picked up by a mail truck twice a day. The truck takes it to the post office where people use machines to sort it and send it to its destination. Most mail goes by air.

In the past the mail went by land in trains or trucks, or it went by sea in ships. In the American West the mail was carried by pony express. In Alaska, reindeer carried the mail. During the 1860s, camels carried the mail in the southern United States.

Before you can mail a letter or package, you need to put stamps on it. The weight of the letter or package tells the post office how many stamps you need. A heavy piece of mail costs more than a light piece of mail. You can mail things in the mailbox or at the post office.

In Canada, letter carriers deliver the mail to people's houses once a day. There is no mail delivery on the weekend. Letter carriers are famous because they promise to deliver the mail in any weather and against any difficulties.

Exercise 3: Read Carefully for Details

Work with a partner. Look in the text for the answers.

1. What colour are mailboxes in Canada?

2. What happens to mail in the post office?

3. List six ways that the mail was carried in the past.

4. What do you need to do before you mail a letter?

5. How does the post office know how many stamps to put on a letter or package?

6. Name two places you can mail a letter.

7. On which days is there no mail delivery in Canada?

8. What promise makes letter carriers famous?

Exercise 4: Review Vocabulary

Find the word that doesn't belong on each line.

1. pick up   eat   deliver   carry

2. horse   truck   camel   reindeer

3. send   mail   sing   post

4. letter   package   envelope   cookie

5. table   truck   train   ship

Did You Know?   The most popular hobby in the world is stamp collecting.

Exercise 5: Practise Grammar

Write the past tense of these verbs.

take

sort

send

go

carry

cost

deliver

put

tell

need

How to Address an Envelope

Exercise 1: Read Carefully for Information

Read the text. Then use the information to address a letter to a friend.

How to Address an Envelope

First, in the middle of the envelope, write the name of the person the letter is for. Use **Mr.** before the name of a man. Use **Mrs.** for a married woman or **Miss** for an unmarried woman. Use **Ms**. for a woman you don't know, a woman you know for business or professional reasons, or a woman who prefers to be called by this title.

Second, under the name, write the address. The address is the street number, the street name and **St., Ave., Rd.** or **Blvd.** These are short forms for the words "street," "avenue," "road" and "boulevard." After the street address, write the apartment number. You can use the symbol # for number; for example: #604. You can also write the apartment number like this: Apt. 604.

Third, under the address, write the name of the city and the province. Put a comma (,) between the city and the province. Each Canadian province has a code with two letters. For example, Nova Scotia is NS, and British Columbia is BC.

Fourth, under the city and province, write the postal code. In Canada, postal codes have six parts, like this: letter, number, letter; number, letter, number; for example: H3T 1J6.

Finally, on the top left-hand corner or back of the envelope, write your address. The stamp goes on the front of the envelope, in the top right-hand corner.

Exercise 2: Read Carefully for Details

Work with a partner. Look in the text for the answers.

1. What does the title "Ms." tell you?

2. What does "Rd." mean in an address?

3. What are two ways to write "Apartment 1523"?

4. How do you give the name of a province on an envelope?

5. Make up two postal codes.

6. What are two places that you can write the return address?

7. Where do you put the stamp?

 # Provinces

Write the abbreviation for each province and territory of Canada as your teacher reads it.

British Columbia

Alberta

Saskatchewan

Manitoba

Ontario

Quebec

New Brunswick

Prince Edward Island

Nova Scotia

Newfoundland

Yukon

Northwest Territories

At the Post Office

Listening Activity 7

Exercise 1: Get Ready to Listen

Before you begin, cover Exercise 4 on page 65.

Read these questions aloud with a partner. What do you think this conversation will be about?

1. The woman wants to:
   a) mail a letter
   b) mail a package
   c) buy stamps

2. She wants stamps for:
   a) Canada and overseas
   b) Canada and the US
   c) The US and overseas

3. All together she buys:
   a) five stamps
   b) six stamps
   c) seven stamps

4. The cost is:
   a) $2.20
   b) $3.20
   c) $3.50

5. Her change is:
   a) $1.50
   b) $1.60
   c) $1.80

Exercise 2: Listen for Meaning

Listen to the conversation. What is the conversation about?

Exercise 3: Listen for Details

Go back to the questions. While you listen, choose the correct answers.

Exercise 4: Listen for Sounds

While you listen, write the missing words.

At the Post Office

Clerk: Can I help you?

Woman: Yes, I'____ like to buy some stamps.

Clerk: For Canada or overseas?

Woman: I'd like four stamps ____ Canada, and two for overseas.

Clerk: OK, here you are. Four for Canada, and two for overseas. That comes ____ $3.20.

Woman: Here's ____ five.

Clerk: And here'____ your change, $1.80.

Woman: Thanks.

Clerk: You'____ welcome.

Exercise 5: Practise Speaking

☐☐ Practise reading the dialogue with a partner. Then change roles and read it again.

Unit 9

Transportation

Bus, Train or Plane
Interaction

Transportation in the City
Reading

What About You?
Discussion

Transportation in Different Cities
Writing

The World's Meanest Taxi Driver
Dictation

Taxi! Taxi!
Listening Activity 8

Saying Addresses
Pronunciation
Writing

How to Take a Bus
Interaction

The Simple Past Tense
Grammar

Max Takes the Bus
Writing

Bus, Train or Plane

There are many ways to travel. You can walk, drive a car or take a taxi. You can take a subway or a bus. If you want to travel further, you can take a train, a boat or a plane.

Work in a group. Look at the picture. Discuss the best way to do the following:

1. Take a tour of the city.
2. Go to a different part of the city.
3. Go to a distant city quickly.
4. Move your furniture to a new apartment.
5. Travel across the ocean.
6. See the countryside when you travel to another city.
7. Visit your friend who lives six blocks away.
8. Go downtown in a hurry when you don't have a car.

Transportation in the City

📖 **Exercise 1: Read Quickly for General Ideas**

Transportation in the City

In different cities, people have different ways to move around. In countries like China, bicycles are a popular kind of transport. Many Chinese ride bicycles to work. Sometimes people use bicycles to carry furniture across town or to carry animals to market.

In Vancouver, many people travel by bus. People sometimes travel by water too. Some people go to work by sea-bus. They can even take a transfer and change from the sea-bus to the city bus.

In cold cities like Toronto or Moscow, people use the subway to stay warm underground. But hot cities such as Singapore have subways too. Subways are a good way to avoid traffic in the streets.

📖 **Exercise 2: Read Carefully for Details**

Work with a partner. Look in the text for the answers.

1. List three ways the Chinese use bicycles.

2. Why do people in Vancouver sometimes need a transfer?

3. Why do people in Toronto and Moscow like the subway?

4. Why do people in Singapore like the subway?

What About You?

Discuss these questions in a group.

1. What are some ways to travel in other cities?

2. What is your favourite way to travel?

3. Interview three students in your class. Find out the cost of transportation in other cities they know about. Make a chart similar to the one below. Write the information on the chart.

	Student A	Student B	Student C
Bus			
Subway			
Transfer needed (yes/no)			
Taxi			
Other			

Transportation in Different Cities

Write about transportation in a city that you know.

The World's Meanest Taxi Driver

There is a taxi driver in New York who is very rude. He smokes a cigar in the taxi. He always drives very fast. He asks for extra money. If people don't want to pay extra, he yells at them.

Taxi! Taxi!

Listening Activity 8

Exercise 1: Get Ready to Listen

☐ ☐ Read the questions aloud with a partner. What do you think the conversation will be about?

1. The woman wants to go to:
   a) Clark Street
   b) Park Street
   c) Clear Street

2. The street is:
   a) far away
   b) not far away
   c) a block away

3. The taxi driver:
   a) went to the right place
   b) got lost
   c) forgot to turn left

4. The woman is:
   a) in a hurry
   b) going shopping
   c) meeting her friend

⊙⊙ Exercise 2: Listen for Meaning

Listen to the conversation. What is the conversation about?

⊙⊙ Exercise 3: Listen for Details

Go back to the questions. While you listen, choose the correct answers.

⊙⊙ Exercise 4: Listen for Sounds

While you listen, write the missing words.

Taxi! Taxi!

Taxi driver: Yes, Ma'am. Where do you want ＿＿ go?

Woman: I want to go to Clark Street, ＿＿ Clark Street.

Taxi driver: Clark Street? Where is Clark Street?

Woman: Clark Street ＿＿ far away. Turn left at the next corner. Then go straight for five blocks. When you get to Maple Street, turn right. Go one more block. The building is at the corner of Maple Street and Clark Street.

Taxi driver: OK, Ma'am. I turn left, then straight ＿＿ five blocks, then right. No problem.

Woman: Stop! You went too far. You forgot ＿＿ turn left at the corner.

Taxi driver: I forgot to turn left? No problem. ＿＿ turn the car around.

Woman: You can't turn the car around. This is a one-way street.

Taxi driver: I'll go around ＿＿ corner.

Woman: That will take too long. I have ＿＿ appointment in ten minutes.

Taxi Driver: I'll go as fast ＿＿ I can.

Woman: Forget it. I'll walk. It'＿＿ be faster.

Exercise 5: Practise Speaking

☐ ☐ Practise reading the dialogue with a partner. Then change roles and read it again.

Saying Addresses

We say street numbers such as 5372 like this:

  fifty-three seventy-two

  OR

  five three seven two

Write the numbers in these addresses in words. Write each in two ways.

  1569 Regent Street

  7856 Bloom Road

  3893 Halpern Street

  9229 Webster Street

  861 Jane Street

  7686 Wellington Avenue

Write the street numbers in these addresses:

Fifty-six ninety-nine Cavendish Boulevard

Twenty-one fourteen Bank Road

Eighteen forty-four Page Street

Ninety-six sixty-six Tupper Street

Fourteen fifty-seven Jupiter Street

Twenty-six seventy-two Maplewood Avenue

How To Take A Bus

Work with a partner to put these steps in order.

1. Sit down on a seat.

2. Look for a bus stop.

3. Put the ticket or money in the fare box.

4. Watch for your stop.

5. Pull the cord to ring the bell.

6. Get a transfer from the driver.

7. Get onto the bus.

8. Get off the bus.

74

The Simple Past Tense

Exercise 1: Regular Simple Past Tense

Here are some present tense verbs. Write the simple past tense of each.

pull

change

enter

move

arrive

transfer

ask

watch

listen

travel

Exercise 2: Irregular Simple Past Tense

Here are some present tense verbs. Write the irregular past tense of each.

take

put

go

run

ride

get

ring

sit

give

buy

Max Takes the Bus

Use the sentences from "How to Take a Bus" (page 73) to write a short story. Use the past tense.

Example: Max looked for a bus stop. He ...

Now underline the past tense verbs you have used. How many are regular? How many are irregular?

Unit 10

Food

Meals in Canada

Exercise 1: Get Ready to Read

Work in a group. Look at the pictures.

1. Name the meals people eat in Canada. At what time do people eat each meal?

2. Name the foods you see in the pictures.

Exercise 2: Read Carefully for Information

Work with a partner. Read the text and then answer the questions.

Meals in Canada

What do you eat every day? Most Canadians eat three meals. Breakfast is in the morning, lunch is around noon (12:00 p.m.) and supper, which is sometimes called dinner, is around 6:00 p.m. Many people also have a snack in the middle of the morning or the middle of the afternoon. When they are at work, this snack is called a coffee break.

What do you eat in a typical meal? For breakfast in Canada, people often have juice or a fruit, and then some toast and coffee. Many people also like to eat cereal with milk, eggs, bacon or pancakes for breakfast. For snacks, some people have fruit or a cup of coffee or tea with a donut. For lunch, people usually eat a sandwich, soup or a salad. They sometimes go out for a hamburger, hotdog or pizza. Students and people who work either bring their lunch with them or go to a cafeteria or restaurant to buy lunch.

For supper, people often have soup with bread to begin the meal. A typical Canadian meal usually has meat, chicken or fish. It often has some kind of vegetable or salad, and also potatoes or rice. For dessert, people sometimes have pie or cake or fruit. They have coffee or tea to finish the meal.

1. At what time do people eat these meals?
   a) breakfast
   b) lunch
   c) supper or dinner

2. When do people have snacks?

3. What foods do people eat at these meals?
   a) breakfast
   b) lunch
   c) supper or dinner

78

Exercise 3: Exchange Information

Make a chart similar to the one below. Interview three students. Write the information on your chart.

	Student A	Student B	Student C
Name			
Number of meals each day			
Numbers of snacks			
Breakfast			
Time			
Foods			
Lunch			
Time			
Foods			
Supper/Dinner			
Time			
Foods			
Snacks			
Times			
Foods			

Exercise 4: Practise Grammar

Adverbs of Frequency

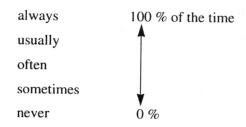

always   100 % of the time

usually

often

sometimes

never   0 %

Find the adverbs of frequency in the text "Meals in Canada" (page 77). Then write out the parts of the sentence with the adverb of frequency.

Example: Supper is sometimes called dinner.

Exercise 5: Practise Spelling

Put the letters in the right order to find the names of foods and drinks.

Example: lsdaa   salad

1. eecfof
2. iejuc
3. eta
4. lmki
5. tsoat
6. trfiu
7. drbae
8. iep
9. psou
10. acke

Don't Get Confused

Your teacher will read some words. What word did you hear?

1. a) soup
    b) soap

2. a) mail
    b) meal

3. a) snake
    b) snack

4. a) lunch
    b) launch

5. a) coke
    b) cake

6. a) tea
    b) tie

Vegetables

Exercise 1: Get Ready to Read

Work with a partner. Look at the picture.

1. Name as many vegetables as you can.
2. Name some things we can put on a salad.
3. Name some vegetables we eat raw, cooked and in a salad.

Exercise 2: Read Carefully for Information

Read the text carefully. Then work with a partner to answer the questions.

Vegetables

In Canada we have many different kinds of vegetables. We eat vegetables in different ways. We often eat them raw. In a salad, for example, we combine vegetables. We put in lettuce, sliced cucumber, green pepper, tomato and many other things.

Canadians often add a salad dressing to their salad. There are many kinds of salad dressings. Some are made with oil and vinegar. Others have mayonnaise or sour cream in them.

At parties, we sometimes cut up vegetables and eat them raw with a dip. A dip is like salad dressing. It can be made of mayonnaise or sour cream and some spices.

There are some vegetables that we always cook. Potatoes and corn are examples. Other vegetables are good raw, but we also cook them. Carrots, onions, broccoli and cauliflower can be cooked alone or can be added to a stew. Mushrooms and green pepper are good in spaghetti sauce.

1. What do we do with vegetables to make a salad?

2. What do Canadians often add to salads?

3. Give two examples of salad dressing.

4. What is a dip?

5. Where is a dip usually served?

6. Name some ingredients of spaghetti sauce.

Exercise 3: Review Vocabulary

□ □ Look at the pictures of vegetables. Make a chart similar to the one below. First write the name of each vegetable. Then check (✔) if the vegetable is usually eaten raw, cooked or both ways.

	Name of vegetable	Raw	Cooked	Both ways
1	cucumber	✔		
2				
3				
4				
5				
6				
7				
8				
9				
10				

A Salad

Exercise 1: Get Ready

Read the list of ingredients for a salad.

Ingredients for Salad	Ingredients for Salad Dressing
1 cucumber	200 ml oil
2 tomatoes	125 ml vinegar
1 head of lettuce	dash of pepper
5 mushrooms	dash of salt
1 green pepper	
1/2 onion	
1 carrot	

Exercise 2: Transfer Information

☐☐ Work with a partner. Look at the pictures.

1. Choose the verb for each picture.
2. Make a chart similar to the one on page 83.
3. From the list of ingredients, put in all the foods that match the actions.

Action	Ingredients
peel	onion, carrot
wash	
slice	
chop	
tear	lettuce
mix	
measure	
pour	

How to Make a Salad

Listening Activity 9

 ## Listen for Information

Here are five steps to make a salad. While you listen, put the steps in order.

1. Mix the salad dressing.
2. Wash the vegetables.
3. Toss the salad.
4. Prepare the vegetables.
5. Pour the dressing onto the salad.

Recipe Exchange

Exercise 1: Get Ready

Prepare a recipe for something you like to eat. List the ingredients. Then write the instructions.

84

Exercise 2: Exchange Information

In a group, explain your recipe to other students.

Fruit in Canada

We grow many kinds of fruit in Canada. Fruit trees grow leaves and flowers in spring. The fruit is ripe (ready to eat) in the summer or fall. In the winter, we import our fresh fruit. Some fruits grow in Canada in summer, and are imported in winter. Imported fruits come from different countries.

Look at the pictures. Work in your group. First describe the fruits. Talk about colour, size, shape, etc. Then complete a chart similar to the one below. Which fruits grow in Canada? Which fruits are imported? Where do the imported fruits come from?

		Fruit	From Canada	Imported	Place
1		avocado		✔	Mexico
2		pineapple		✔	Hawaii
3					
4					
5					
6					
7					
8					
9					
10					
11					
12					

A /An

Practise Pronunciation

Use **a** before a consonant. Use **an** before a vowel.

Examples: **a** grape, **an** apricot

Choose **a** or **an** to use before each word:

apple	pineapple
banana	cucumber
grapefruit	onion
avocado	carrot
kiwi	mushroom
orange	tomato
pear	watermelon
egg	potato

Sandwiches

Exercise 1: Read Quickly for General Ideas

Sandwiches

What do you eat when you are in a hurry or when you feel lazy? Many Canadians eat a sandwich. The most famous sandwich is the hamburger, but the hamburger isn't a real sandwich. A real sandwich is two pieces of bread with something in the middle. The bread can be plain or toasted.

You can put many things between the pieces of bread. Cheese is good. Tuna, salmon and chicken are popular. You can add raw vegetables like lettuce, cucumber and tomatoes. You can even add fruit. Peanut butter and banana sandwiches are popular with children. Bacon, lettuce and tomato sandwiches are popular with adults. We call these sandwiches "BLTs." To make BLTs, we put mayonnaise on the bread before we add the bacon, lettuce and tomato.

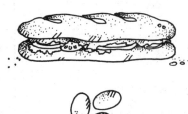

86

Exercise 2: Read Carefully for Details

Work with a partner. Look in the text for the answers.

1. When do Canadians eat sandwiches?
2. What is the most famous sandwich?
3. What does a real sandwich have?
4. List six things you can put in a sandwich.
5. Which fruit is used in sandwiches?
6. Name a sandwich that children really like.
7. What is a BLT?
8. Explain how to make a BLT.

Exercise 3: Review Vocabulary

1. Which word doesn't belong?

   lettuce   banana   cucumber   tomato

2. Name two kinds of fish.

3. Find words that mean the opposite:

   slow

   toasted

   cooked

   children

Did You Know?   Milk is a common drink in Canada. Most children and many adults drink milk. In other parts of the world, people do not drink milk. Many people from other countries are surprised to see people drink milk in Canada.

Packages in the Supermarket

Work with a partner. Look at the pictures. Use the words under the pictures to complete the expressions.

1. a _____ of eggs
2. a _____ of oil
3. a _____ of mayonnaise
4. a _____ of potatoes
5. a _____ of cookies
6. a _____ of margarine
7. a _____ of cereal
8. a _____ of soup
9. a _____ of milk
10. a _____ of tuna
11. a _____ of potato chips
12. a _____ of toilet paper

Jar	Bottle	Carton	Can	Container
Bag	Package	Box	Sack	Roll

The Supermarket

Listening Activity 10

Exercise 1: Get Ready to Listen

Before you begin, cover Exercise 4 on page 89.

Work with a partner. Look at the plan of the supermarket.

1. How many aisles are there?
2. What is next to the oranges?
3. What is to the right of the meat?
4. What is to the left of the eggs?
5. Are soft drinks on the left side or the right side of Aisle 4?
6. Is the coffee on the left side or the right side of Aisle 3?
7. Where is the frozen food?

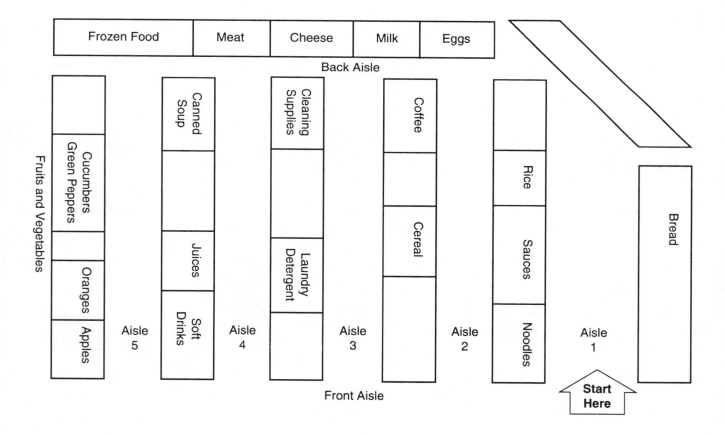

Exercise 2: Listen for Information

Listen to the conversations. As you listen, follow the route.

○○ Exercise 3: Listen for Information Again

While you listen, write the names of the things you find.

Exercise 4: Practise Speaking

☐☐ Practise reading these dialogues with a partner. Change roles and read it again.

The Supermarket

1. **Woman:** Excuse me. I want a head of lettuce. Where can I find it please?

    Clerk: It's in Aisle 5, near the back. Go to the back aisle and turn left. Then go to the last aisle. At the last aisle, turn left again. I think it's the first table.

    Woman: Towards the back. OK. Thanks a lot.

2. **Man:** Can you help me? I want some tea. Where is the tea?

    Clerk: Oh, sure. I know. It's near the coffee. Walk down the front aisle. Go to Aisle 3. Turn right. The tea is between the coffee and the cereal.

    Man: Thanks. Thanks a lot.

3. **Man:** Hi. Where is the oil please? I can't find it.

    Clerk: Oil, oil? Oh yeah. Go to the back aisle. Turn left. At Aisle 2, turn left again. It's next to the rice.

    Man: Thanks. I need the oil for a salad.

    Clerk: Huh? Oh, sure. Enjoy your salad.

4. **Woman:** Excuse me. I'd like to buy a birthday cake. Do you have any?

    Clerk: A birthday cake? Sure. At the bakery. It's at the back of the store. Go to the end of Aisle 1. The bakery is between the bread and the eggs. They have lots of nice cakes there, chocolate, pecan...

    Woman: Thanks. Chocolate is just what I need. It's for my daughter's birthday party. She's turning eight tomorrow.

5. **Man:** I need some soap. Dishwashing soap. Where can I find it?

    Clerk: Oh, the dishwashing soap is near the cleaning supplies. Walk towards the fruit and vegetable section. When you get to Aisle 4, turn right. It's the third section.

    Man: Thank you.

Good to Eat

Crossword Puzzle

Across

4. At 7:00 every morning I eat ____.

6. I have orange ____ for breakfast.

7. I put lettuce and cucumber in my ____.

9. I put ____ on my toast.

12. At 12:00 every day, I eat ____.

13. An ____ is often a red fruit.

Down

1. Every morning I drink hot ____.

2. I eat a peanut butter ____ for lunch.

3. At 6:00 every day I eat ____.

5. I eat ____ and jam for breakfast.

8. I put ____ in my coffee.

10. ____ is a hot drink.

11. At 10:30 every morning I have a ____.

The Body

The Head

Exercise 1: Get Ready

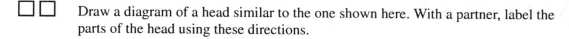

Draw a diagram of a head similar to the one shown here. With a partner, label the parts of the head using these directions.

1. The **nose** is in the middle of the face.
2. The **eyes** are above the nose.
3. Two **ears** are on the sides of the head.
4. The **chin** is under the mouth.
5. The **cheeks** are between the ears and the mouth.
6. The **eyebrows** are above the eyes.
7. The **forehead** is above the eyebrows.
8. The **lips** are around the mouth.

Exercise 2: Use the Information

1. Draw a moustache above the lips.
2. Draw a beard on the chin.
3. Draw long hair on the head.
4. Draw glasses on the face.

Match the Hairstyle

Work with a partner. Look at the pictures of hairstyles. Then find the people in the picture.

Mark's hair is short and straight.

Raoul's hair is short and curly.

Yuki has bangs and long straight hair.

Amy has a ponytail.

Andrea has pigtails.

Melanie has braids.

Miguel has straight hair, a moustache and a beard.

Natalie's hair is wavy.

Maria has a bun.

Paul is bald.

The Haircut

Listening Activity 11

Exercise 1: Get Ready to Listen

□ □ **A.** Look at the picture of people at the hairdresser. With a partner, talk about some things the hairdresser does. For example, a hairdresser cuts hair.

Before you begin, cover Exercise 4 below.

☐ ☐   **B.** Read these questions aloud with a partner. What do you think the conversation will be about?

1. What does Rosa want?
2. Rosa wants her hair short in the back.   **T** (true) or **F** (false)?
3. Rosa wants to have bangs.   **T   F**
4. Rosa's hair is long and straight.   **T   F**
5. The hairdresser doesn't know what to do.   **T   F**
6. Rosa wants her hair to look like her friend's hair.   **T   F**

Exercise 2: Listen for Meaning

Listen to the conversation. What is the conversation about?

Exercise 3: Listen for Details

Go back to the questions. While you listen, answer the questions.

Exercise 4: Listen for Sounds

While you listen, write the missing words.

The Haircut

Hairdresser: Hi. What _____ I do for you?

Rosa: I'_____ like to get my hair cut please.

Hairdresser: Oh, get your hair cut, eh? OK. _____ you want your hair short?

Rosa: Well, not too short. My hair is curly. It doesn't look good too short. Don't cut too much _____ the back.

Hairdresser: Not too short in the back, right! How about _____ front? Do you want it shorter in the front? Do you want bangs?

Rosa: Bangs? No, I _____ like bangs. Don't touch the front.

Hairdresser: I see. No bangs. Don't touch the front. How about the sides? Shall I cut a bit on the sides?

Rosa: Well, just _____ one side. Cut a little on the left side.

Hairdresser: On one side? Are you sure?

Rosa: Yeah! _____ the latest style. All my friends wear it that way. It's really "in."

Hairdresser: OK. You're the boss. But I think it looks kind of weird.

Exercise 5: Practise Speaking

Practise reading the dialogue with a partner. Then change roles and read it again.

Exercise 6: Review Expressions

What do these expressions mean? Match each expression to its meaning.

1. you're the boss
2. it's really in
3. kind of weird
4. don't touch the front
5. yeah
6. eh?

a) strange, unusual
b) it is popular
c) you are the customer
d) right? (am I correct?)
e) yes
f) don't cut the front

In the Drugstore

Exercise 1: Get Ready

The picture shows some of the things you buy in the drugstore. Write the missing words.

1. You need a bottle of _____ to wash your hair.
2. You can use a can of _____ to keep your hair in place.
3. You need a tube of _____ to brush your teeth.
4. You need a box of _____ when you have a cut.
5. You need a can of _____ to shave.
6. You need a box of _____ when you have a cold.
7. You need a bottle of _____ when your hands feel dry.
8. You need a tube of _____ when you have a burn.
9. You need a bottle of _____ before you go out on a hot, sunny day.
10. You need a box of _____ when you have a cough.
11. You need a stick of _____ not to smell bad.

Exercise 2: Review Vocabulary

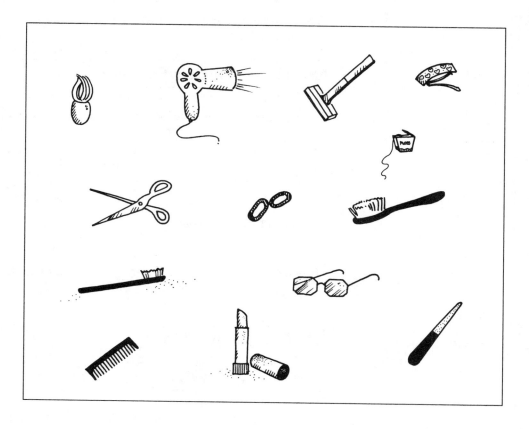

☐☐   Work with a partner. Look at the pictures.

1. Name the objects shown.

2. Make a chart similar to the one below. Show where you use these objects:

**toothbrush   hairbrush   lipstick   nail file   dental floss   glasses
razor   shaving brush   hair dryer   scissors   hair clip   hair elastic
comb**

Hair	Eyes	Teeth	Fingernails	Face (men)	Face (women)
				razor	lipstick

Body Quiz

Exercise 1: Get Ready

Work in a group. Look at the diagrams of body parts. Choose the best answer.

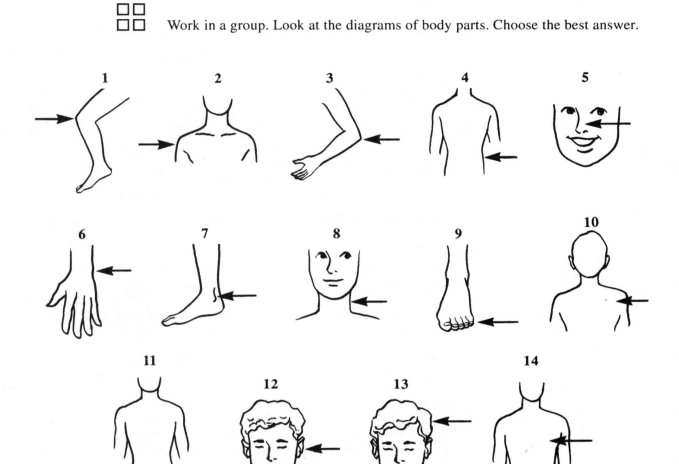

What is ...

1. in the middle of the leg:
   a) the shoulder
   b) the knee
   c) the elbow

2. below the neck:
   a) the head
   b) the ears
   c) the shoulders

98

3. in the middle of the arm:
   a) the neck
   b) the elbow
   c) the hips

4. between the chest and the hips:
   a) the neck
   b) the waist
   c) the legs

5. in the middle of the face:
   a) the ears
   b) the nose
   c) the chin

6. between the hand and the arm:
   a) the waist
   b) the elbow
   c) the wrist

7. between the leg and the foot:
   a) the wrist
   b) the ankle
   c) the elbow

8. below the chin:
   a) the nose
   b) the eyes
   c) the neck

9. on the foot:
   a) the toes
   b) the chest
   c) the wrist

10. behind the chest:
    a) the ears
    b) the hands
    c) the back

11. below the waist:
    a) the hips
    b) the head
    c) the neck

12. on the sides of the head:
    a) the ears
    b) the toes
    c) the fingers

13. on top of the head:
    a) the nose
    b) the waist
    c) the hair

14. Between the neck and the waist:
    a) the hips
    b) the chest
    c) the knee

Did You Know? The human body has 656 muscles. When we smile we use 17 different muscles. When we are angry and we frown we use 43 different muscles.

Exercise 2: Review Vocabulary

Work with a partner. Look at the picture. Write the name of each part.

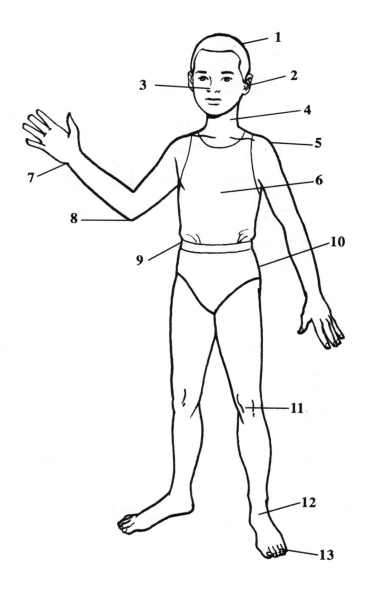

On the Body

Crossword Puzzle

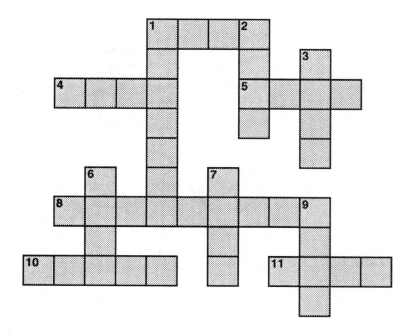

Across

1. We use our _____ to walk.

4. The _____ is at the bottom of the face.

5. We see with our _____.

8. Some men have a _____ above their lips.

10. We have _____ to chew our food.

11. Our hands are at the ends of our _____.

Down

1. We have five _____ on each hand.

2. We have five _____ on each foot.

3. The _____ is below the head.

6. The _____ is in the middle of the face.

7. We have _____ on the top of our heads.

9. We have two _____ on the sides of our head.

Unit 12

The Weather

Weather in Canada

Exercise 1: Get Ready to Read

☐☐   **A.** Work with a partner. Look at the pictures of weather conditions in Canada. Describe the weather condition in each box.

B. Look at the picture of the tree in different seasons in Canada. Write the names of the seasons.

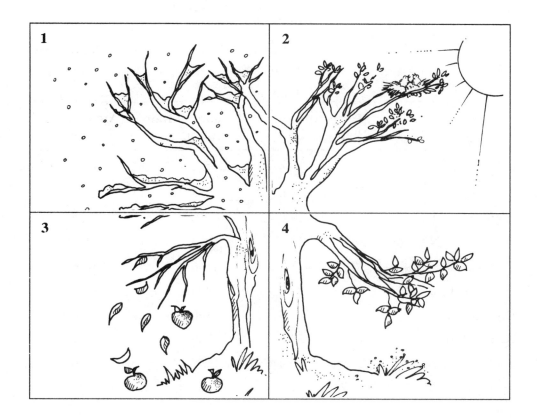

Exercise 2: Read Carefully for Information

Read the text. Then make a chart that shows two things about the weather in each season.

Weather in Canada

Canada has four seasons. They are winter, spring, summer and fall. The seasons are different in different parts of Canada. Victoria and Vancouver have mild weather all year. In other parts of Canada, the summers are very hot and the winters are very cold.

In most of Canada, winter is very cold. The snow and cold weather start in November. They end in April. Spring is short in most of Canada. It lasts from April to June. The weather is warm and sometimes it rains. The summer months are July and August. The summer is hot and humid in some parts of Canada. On the prairies the weather is hot and dry in summer. Autumn (or fall) is from September to November. Autumn weather is cooler. Sometimes it is sunny and sometimes it rains. Autumn is very beautiful. The leaves on the trees change colour. They change from green to red, orange and yellow before they fall off the trees. Autumn is a lovely time of year.

Weather Chart

Exercise 1: Get Ready

Here is weather information about some cities in Canada.

	Temperature		Amount of Rain	Amount of Snow	Amount of Wind
	High	Low	(mm)	(cm)	(km/h)
Calgary, Alta .	31.9	−30.4	404.5	72.8	106
Charlottetown, P.E.I.	30.5	−24.6	1258	334	108
Edmonton, Alta.	31	−29.8	530.6	55	77
Fredericton, N.B.	34	−30	1013	227	83
Halifax, N.S.	30	−21.8	1546.8	136	100
Montreal, Que.	33.4	−28.3	805.2	172	96
Ottawa, Ont.	35.2	−29.8	860.4	186.5	83
Regina, Sask.	40.4	−37	308	77	96
Saint John, N.B.	29.5	−26.4	1357.3	210.7	88
St. John's, Nfld.	27.7	−19.4	1507.4	242.3	116
Toronto, Ont.	37.6	−21.7	647	94.7	96
Vancouver, B.C.	31.7	−8	1255.6	9.6	68
Whitehorse, Yukon	25.2	−37.8	337.8	118.1	83
Winnipeg, Man.	38.4	−32	381.5	110.5	88

Did You Know?	Most Canadians think of summer as the time between two long weekends: July 1, which is Canada Day, and September 1, which is Labour Day. However, summer weather can start in May and continue until mid-September in many parts of Canada.

□□ **Exercise 2: Transfer Information**

Work with a partner. Make a chart similar to the one below. Check (✔) the cities to complete the chart.

City	Highest Temperature	Lowest Temperature	Most Rain	Least Rain	Most Snow	Least Snow	Most Wind	Least Wind
Calgary								
Charlottetown								
Edmonton								
Fredericton								
Halifax								
Montreal								
Ottawa								
Regina	✔							
Saint John								
St. John's								
Toronto								
Vancouver								
Whitehorse								
Winnipeg								

Exercise 3: Review Vocabulary

Match the opposites.

most	lowest
hottest	colder
highest	least
biggest	coldest
warmer	smallest

Exercise 4: Transfer Information

Use your chart to complete these sentences.

Example: St. John's has the most wind.

1. Regina has the ____ temperature.
2. Charlottetown has the most ____.
3. Halifax has the most ____.
4. The city with the least snow is ____.
5. The city with the least wind is ____.
6. The city with the lowest temperature is ____.

Exercise 5: Practise Grammar

Complete the sentences with **more** or **less**.

1. Montreal has ____ snow than Ottawa.
2. Toronto has ____ rain than Vancouver.
3. Regina has ____ wind than Halifax.
4. Fredericton has ____ snow than Regina.
5. Vancouver has ____ rain than Ottawa.
6. Calgary has ____ wind than Regina.

Weather Report

Listening Activity 12

○ ○ **Listen for Details**

Listen to the weather report for Canada on the tape. Look at the map. Put the correct symbol for each city.

Did You Know?   The Inuit are people who live in the Canadian Arctic. They have more than twenty different words for snow. Each word describes a different kind of snow.

Canada

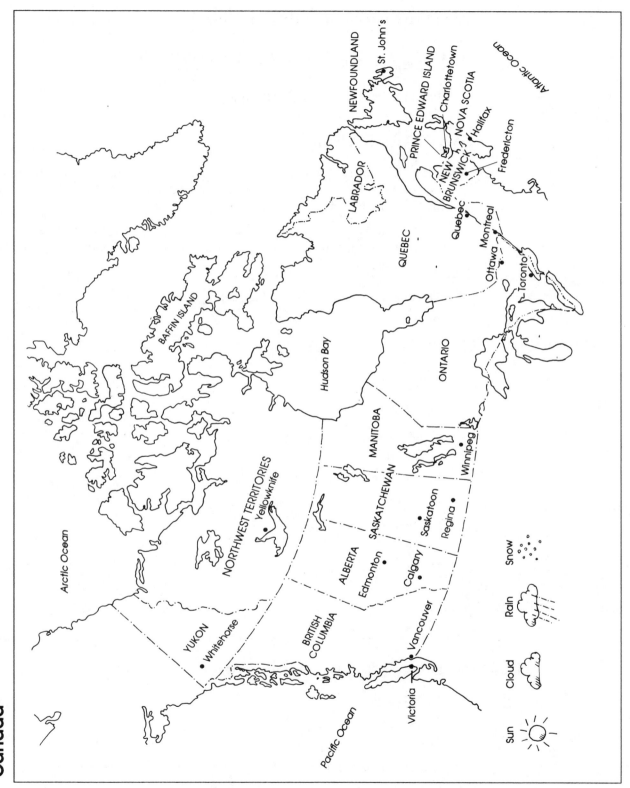

What Does It Mean?

Exercise 1: Read Quickly for General Ideas

Read this paragraph and answer the questions.

What Does It Mean?

You are in Winnipeg. It is January. You listen to the weather report on the radio. The weather report says, "It's a beautiful sunny day today." What do you wear outside? A summer jacket? A winter coat?

In Canada, when the weather reports say "It's a beautiful sunny day," they may mean it's a beautiful, sunny **winter** day. It is sunny, but it is still very cold. You need warm winter clothes.

1. What is the weather like on this January day in Winnipeg?
    a) hot
    b) sunny
    c) cold
    d) windy
    e) rainy

2. What should you wear outside?
    a) a coat
    b) a jacket
    c) shoes
    d) boots
    e) sandals
    f) a T-shirt

Exercise 2: Discuss

In a group, discuss what you think these expressions mean.

1. It's a gorgeous day.
2. The weather is cooling off.
3. Sunny with cloudy periods.
4. Chance of showers.
5. Snow or freezing rain tonight.
6. Have a nice day! (Is this a weather statement at all?)

The Best Time to Travel

Role Play

Partner A

You are visiting your cousin in Canada. This is your first time in Canada. You want to visit four cities in different parts of Canada. Tell your cousin where you want to go, and in which months.

Partner B

You live in Canada. You know all about the weather in summer and winter. Your cousin wants to visit different parts of Canada at different times of the year. Help him or her decide when to go to each place. Talk about the weather in different seasons and places.

Both Partners

Together, write your dialogue. Then act it out for the class. In the dialogue, say where you want to go, and when. Talk about how the weather will be at each place you want to visit at the time you want to go.

What About You?

Discuss these questions in a group.

1. How many seasons are there in other countries?
2. What changes happen in each season?
3. What is the highest temperature? The lowest?
4. What is your favourite season? Why?

Groundhog Day

Choose the correct word for each space.

spring   shadow   day   animal   hole   ground

February 2 is a special ____ in Canada. It is groundhog day. A groundhog is a
                        1

small ____ that lives in a hole in the ____. On February 2, it comes out of its
      2   **3**

hole. If it is a sunny day, the groundhog sees its shadow. It goes back into its

____. This means ____ will not come for a long time. If it is a cloudy day, the
4   **5**

groundhog does not see its ____. The groundhog stays outside. This means
                           6

spring will come soon.

Unit 13

Clothing

What to Wear
Reading
Cultural Information

Tops and Bottoms
Vocabulary

Shopping in a Hurry
Listening Activity 13

Dressing for Winter
Vocabulary

Packing a Suitcase
Interaction
Cultural Information

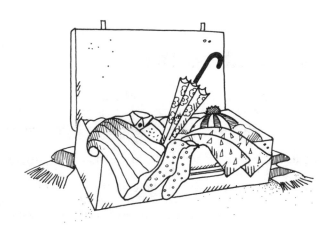

What to Wear

Exercise 1: Get Ready to Read

Work with a partner. Look at the pictures of clothes. How many things can you name?

Exercise 2: Read Quickly for General Ideas

What to Wear

Winter in most parts of Canada is cold. You need warm clothes to keep your body warm. You also need to keep your head, hands and feet warm.

The first thing you need is a heavy coat or jacket. Then you need a warm hat to keep your head and ears warm. To keep your hands warm, you need gloves or mitts. A scarf keeps your neck warm. When it is very cold, you can cover your mouth and nose with your scarf.

Winter boots are very important to keep your feet warm. Try to get waterproof boots. Then your feet will not get wet if you step in a puddle.

Under your jacket or coat, you also need warm clothes. You need shirts and sweaters with long sleeves. You need long pants and you need warm socks.

Summer in Canada is hot. You need light clothes to keep your body cool. You do not need a coat or jacket every day. You need a light coat or jacket, or a raincoat, for rainy days. Rain boots are also useful because the rain in Canada is cold, even in the summer.

In the summer, you need shirts or tops with short sleeves. For work or class, women usually wear a skirt and top, pants and a top, or a dress. Men often wear short-sleeved shirts and light pants to work. After work, many people wear shorts and T-shirts.

On their feet, women wear shoes or sandals to work or class. Men usually wear socks and shoes. After work, men and women often wear sandals or sneakers (running shoes).

Exercise 3: Read Carefully for Details

Work with a partner. Look in the text for the answers.

1. Why do you need warm clothes in Canada?
2. What is the most important piece of clothing to have in the winter?
3. Why is a hat important?
4. Name two things you can do with a scarf.
5. What should you look for when you buy winter boots?
6. Name two items of clothing with long sleeves.
7. Why are rain boots useful in Canada?
8. What do women wear to work in the summer?
9. What do men wear to work in the summer?
10. What do people wear after work?
11. What do people wear on their feet when they go to work?
12. What do they often wear on their feet after work?

Exercise 4: Review Vocabulary

Make a list of clothes that are named in the text. List them under **Winter** or **Summer**. Some items might be listed under both winter and summer.

Tops and Bottoms

☐☐ Where do you wear these items? Make a chart similar to the one below. Work with a partner. Write the items on the chart.

belt socks ring bracelet T-shirt cap pants sneakers boots skirt jacket coat sweater vest watch slippers sun-hat necklace raincoat high heels sandals woollen hat blouse shirt sweatshirt tie gloves mittens

Example: On your waist: belt

	On your hands				
	On your head				
	On your feet				
	On your neck				
	On your upper body				
	On your lower body				
	On your wrist				
	On top of your clothes				

Did You Know?   In some elementary and high schools in Canada, students wear uniforms or have a dress code. For example, students may wear a special school colour. In other schools, and in colleges and universities, students wear what they like. Many students of all ages like to wear jeans, T-shirts and sweatshirts to school.

Shopping in a Hurry

Listening Activity 13

Exercise 1: Get Ready to Listen

Before you begin, cover Exercise 4 on page 115.

☐ ☐ **A.** Work with a partner. Look at the pictures. What do you think the conversation will be about?

B. Read the questions aloud with a partner.

1. What does the woman want to buy?
2. What colour does she try on?
3. What size does she wear?
4. She goes to the fitting room. **T** (true) or **F** (false)?
5. The dress doesn't fit her. **T F**
6. She pays cash. **T F**

Exercise 2: Listen for Meaning

Listen to the conversation. What is the conversation about?

Exercise 3: Listen for Details

Go back to the questions. While you listen, write the answers.

Exercise 4: Listen for Sounds

While you listen, write the missing words.

Shopping in a Hurry

Woman: I need a new dress. I'm in a big hurry. What ____ you have?

Sales clerk: I have this dress. ____ very nice. It comes in blue or red.

Woman: I ____ try the red one. What size is it?

Sales clerk: I have it in size 9 and size 11. What size ____ you wear?

Woman: I wear size 11. I'll try ____ on.

Sales clerk: That's fine. The fitting rooms are on the left.

Woman: The fitting rooms? I don't have time to go to the fitting rooms. I'm in a big hurry. I'll try it on over my skirt and blouse.

Sales clerk: You'____ try it on over your skirt and blouse?

Woman: Yes! See, it fits perfectly! I'____ take it.

Sales clerk: That'____ very good, Ma'am. Will that be cash or charge?

Woman: Charge it. 'Bye.

Sales clerk: 'Bye. Boy, that was ____ fastest shopping I ever saw!

Exercise 5: Practise Speaking

Practise reading the dialogue with a partner. Then change roles and read it again.

Dressing for Winter

Choose the correct word for each space.

heated   bus   coat   cold   shirt

When it is very ____ (1) outside, it is important to dress warmly. It is also important to remember that when you go into a building, a store, a ____ (2) or the subway, it is very warm. Buildings and stores are ____ (3) to summer temperatures. It is a good idea to wear layers of clothes, such as a ____ (4) and a sweater under your coat. That way you can take off your ____ (5) and sweater when you feel too warm.

Packing a Suitcase

Express Yourself

Work in a group. Plan a trip to another part of Canada.

1. Decide where you want to go, and at what time of the year.
2. Make a list of things you will pack in your suitcase. Make sure you have the clothes you need for the climate and for the activities you will do.

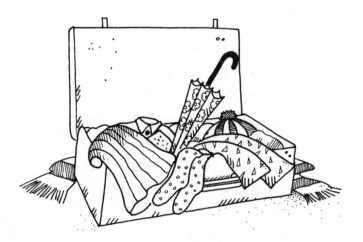

Unit 14

Animals

Quiz on Animals

Exercise 1: Get Ready

Look at the pictures of the animals. Work in a group to name the animals.

Exercise 2: Practise Vocabulary

What do you know about these animals? Read the questions and choose the correct answers. More than one answer can be correct.

Example: An elephant has:

    a) claws

    b) a trunk

    c) knees

    Answer: a trunk and knees

1. A giraffe has a long:
   a) tail
   b) neck
   c) trunk

2. A polar bear is:
   a) brown
   b) black
   c) white

3. A tiger has sharp:
   a) claws
   b) teeth
   c) fins

4. A camel has:
   a) wings
   b) a hump
   c) a tail

5. A monkey has:
    a) a long tail
    b) a short tail
    c) long legs and arms

6. A kangaroo has:
    a) a trunk
    b) a long tail
    c) a pouch

7. A fish has:
    a) legs
    b) arms
    c) fins

8. A bird has:
    a) wings
    b) feathers
    c) a beak

9. A rabbit has:
    a) long ears
    b) fur
    c) paws

10. A turtle has:
    a) fur
    b) a shell
    c) tusks

11. An alligator has:
    a) a large mouth
    b) a long tail
    c) wings

12. A beaver has:
    a) feathers
    b) fur
    c) a large tail

13. A rabbit can be:
    a) red
    b) white
    c) blue

14. An elephant has:
    a) big eyes
    b) big ears
    c) fur

15. A polar bear has:
    a) feathers
    b) fins
    c) fur

16. A camel is:
    a) brown
    b) green
    c) red

Which Animal Is This?

Exercise 1: Get Ready to Read

☐ ☐ Work with a partner. Look at the animals in the picture. How many can you name?

Exercise 2: Read Carefully for Information

Read the descriptions of some animals. Find each animal in the list below. You can look back at the other pictures of animals to help you.

**monkey   penguin   rabbit   kangaroo   bear   cow   frog   beaver
horse   whale   lion   elephant   mouse**

Which Animal Is This?

1. This animal is very big. Its height is 2 metres. It weighs about 100 kilograms. It has a small head with large ears. It has strong legs and a strong tail. This animal jumps very well and it runs fast. It eats vegetables. When this animal has a baby, the baby lives in a pouch on the mother's stomach for almost a year. This animal lives in Australia.

2. This animal can grow to be 32 metres long and can weigh 150 tonnes. It has a large tail and fins. It lives in the water but it breathes air. It swims and dives well. It eats fish and plants. This animal travels a lot. In summer, it goes to cold waters to feed. In winter, it goes to warm waters to breed. This is the biggest animal in the world.

3. This animal is big. It is black, brown or white. It has horns on its head and it has a tail. It lives on a farm. This animal gives us milk to drink. We also use this animal to get meat. The meat from this animal is called beef.

4. This animal is very useful for people. It is a big animal and it is strong. It can run very fast. Before people had cars, they used this animal for transportation. Now people ride this animal for sport. People also like to race this animal. This animal is useful on farms. It can pull machinery.

5. This animal is a little bigger than a cat. It has long arms and legs and a long tail. It lives in the jungle. It swings from trees by its hands, and it hangs from trees by its tail. It can move very fast. We can often see this animal in a zoo or at a circus.

6. This animal lives in Canada and the United States. It lives in lakes and ponds in the woods. It has sharp front teeth. It has fur and a long, flat tail. This animal is a very good swimmer. It is a very hard worker. It cuts down trees to make its home. This animal's picture is on the Canadian nickel.

Exercise 3: Read Carefully for Details

Read the text again. Which words in each paragraph helped you find the answers?

Big and Small

Listening Activity 14

Exercise 1: Get Ready to Listen

Work in a group. Read the questions and discuss them.

Which animal:

1. is the biggest in the world?
2. can live longer than people?
3. is the tallest in the world?
4. is the fastest land animal?
5. is the fastest bird?
6. has the largest ears?
7. is the most intelligent?

Exercise 2: Listen For Details

Go back to the questions. While you listen, write the answers.

Where Animals Live

Animals live everywhere in the world. Some animals live on land. They can live on mountains, in forests or in jungles. Other animals live in water. They can live in oceans or in lakes, ponds or rivers.

Exercise 1: Get Ready

Work in a group. Look at the pictures of places where animals live. Which words describe the climate in each place?

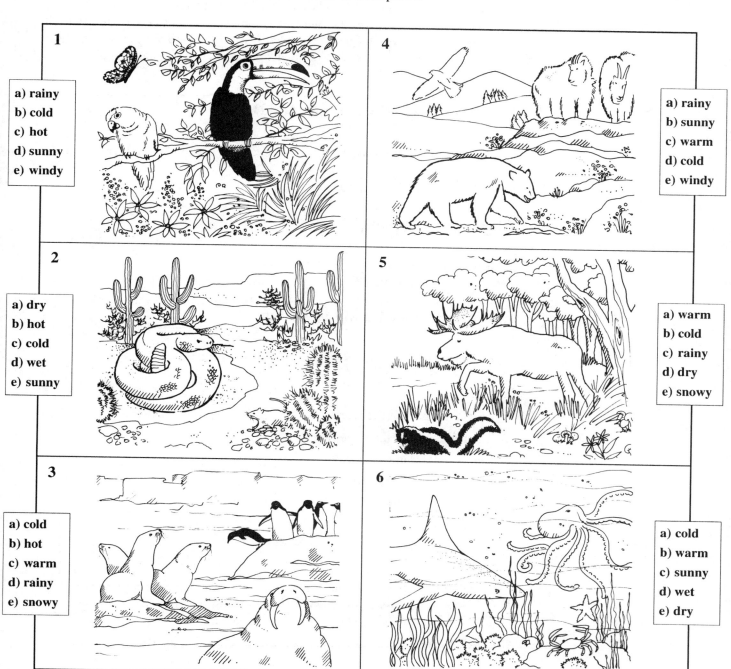

1
a) rainy
b) cold
c) hot
d) sunny
e) windy

4
a) rainy
b) sunny
c) warm
d) cold
e) windy

2
a) dry
b) hot
c) cold
d) wet
e) sunny

5
a) warm
b) cold
c) rainy
d) dry
e) snowy

3
a) cold
b) hot
c) warm
d) rainy
e) snowy

6
a) cold
b) warm
c) sunny
d) wet
e) dry

Exercise 2: Use the Information

Make a chart similar to the one below. Work in a group. Put the name of each animal in the correct place. Some animals live in more than one place.

**penguin   whale   tiger   monkey   bird   fish   camel   squirrel   deer
rabbit   turtle   walrus   seal   raccoon   frog   mouse   snake
moose   bear   goat**

Jungle	Mountain	Ocean	Forest	Desert	Polar Region

What Can It Do?

Animals can do many different things. Different animals have special features that help them. For example, an elephant can pick up a tree with its trunk.

Match the animal with the thing it can do.

1. giraffe   give milk
2. camel   talk
3. monkey   hide in the grass
4. beaver   eat leaves from the top of a tree
5. kangaroo   drink 20 litres of water at once
6. tiger   pick up objects with its hands
7. polar bear   carry its baby on its stomach
8. cow   use its tail to build a house
9. parrot   hide in the snow

Did You Know?   Beavers work very hard. They cut down trees to make their home. In a year, one beaver can down down 215 trees. That is why when someone is very busy, we say he or she is "busy as a beaver."

Animals in the City

Exercise 1: Get Ready to Discuss

Work with a partner. Look at the pictures of animals that live in the city. Then read the descriptions of four animals. Write the names of the animals described.

1. This animal has small ears and eyes. It has an enormous bushy tail.

2. This animal has a mask and a long tail.

3. This animal lives outside in many cities. In North America, it is a popular pet.

4. This animal flies. It lands on your balcony or your window sill.

| Raccoon | Cat | Squirrel | Pigeon |

Exercise 2: Discuss

Discuss these questions in a group.

1. What animals do you see in the city in Canada?

2. What are some animals you find in the city in other places?

3. Name some city animals that people like, and some city animals that people don't like.

Where Do You Find Them?

Exercise 1: Read to Increase Speed

Work with a partner. Read one paragraph and stop. See if you can answer the questions. Do not write the answers yet. Then read the second paragraph in the same way, and then the third.

Where Do You Find Them?

The most common animals we find in the city in Canada are dogs and cats. <u>They</u> are popular indoor pets. But we often see <u>them</u> outside too. Cats like to walk in gardens and alleys. Dogs like to walk in the streets or run in the park. Some people have birds and fish as pets, too. The birds and fish live in houses and
5   apartments where we don't see <u>them</u>.

Cities have other animals too. <u>These</u> animals aren't pets. They can even be pests. Pigeons live in many cities and <u>they</u> aren't always popular. They can make a mess on apartment balconies or on the streets. A more popular city animal is the squirrel. We see <u>it</u> playing in the park and running up trees. Many people say that
10   <u>it</u> is cute.

People who live near the woods or parks can have strange visitors. These visitors are raccoons. Raccoons are bigger than cats. At night, <u>they</u> come near houses to look for food in the garbage. People think <u>they</u> are pests. City workers
14   sometimes come and take the raccoons away.

Paragraph 1

1. Name four animals we find in the city.

2. Where do cats like to walk?

3. Where do dogs like to walk?

4. Where do some animals live?

Paragraph 2

5. Name an animal in the city that is not a pet.

6. Where do pigeons make a mess?

7. Where do squirrels live?

8. Why do people like squirrels?

Paragraph 3

9. How big are raccoons?

10. What do they do at night?

Exercise 2: Read Carefully for Details

Read the text again carefully. Then go back to the questions and write the answers.

Exercise 3: Contextual Reference

What do the underlined words refer to?

Example: In line 1 they refers to dogs and cats.

1. In line 2 them refers to _____ .

2. In line 5 them refers to _____ .

3. In line 6 these refers to _____ .

4. In line 7 they refers to _____ .

5. In line 9 it refers to _____ .

6. In line 10 it refers to _____ .

7. In line 12 they refers to _____ .

8. In line 13 they refers to _____ .

Unit 15

Eating In/Eating Out

Sunday Dinner
Listening Activity 15

Kinds of Restaurants
Reading
Cultural Information

Paying the Bill
Listening Activity 16

MENU
HAMBURGER   COKE
HOT DOG   7 UP
FRENCH FRIES   COOKIES

Sunday Dinner

Listening Activity 15

Patrick's family is having Sunday dinner. They have a guest. Jie is from China. Patrick and Jie are at the end of the table. They are talking about the meal.

Exercise 1: Get Ready to Listen

Before you begin, cover Exercise 4 on page 129.

☐☐ **A.** Work with a partner. Look at the picture. Name the things on the table.

plate
spoon
dish
bowl
fork
glass
knife
basket

☐☐ **B.** Read these sentences aloud with a partner. Some are true, some are false. What do you think the conversation will be about?

1. Patrick and Jie are hungry.

2. The meal is roast chicken.

3. Patrick's father will serve the meat.

4. The dish of peas and carrots is on the right.

5. Gravy is to put on the meat.

6. The bread is on a plate.

7. You put butter on the bread.

8. The family will have cheese for dessert.

⊙⊙ **Exercise 2: Listen for Meaning**

Listen to the conversation. What is the conversation about?

⊙⊙ **Exercise 3: Listen for Details**

Go back to the sentences. While you listen, write **T** (true) or **F** (false).

⊙⊙ **Exercise 4: Listen for Sounds**

While you listen, write the missing words.

Sunday Dinner

Jie: Thanks for the invitation Patrick. The food looks great! _____ starving.

Patrick: Me too. I'm really hungry.

Jie: Excuse me Patrick, but what kind of meat is on the large plate?

Patrick: It's roast beef. Dad will cut it. Then _____ serve everyone a piece.

Jie: Oh. What's in the two bowls? _____ looks hot.

Patrick: Those bowls have vegetables in them. The dish on the right _____ hot peas and carrots. The big bowl has potatoes in _____.

Jie: What about the big cup with the spoon beside it?

Patrick: It's gravy. You _____ put it on your meat or on your potatoes.

Jie: Is that bread _____ the basket?

Patrick: Yes. And the small dish is butter. It's to put on the bread.

Jie: That's a big meal.

Patrick: Today we'_____ have dessert too. My father made a cheesecake.

Jie: Cheese?

Patrick: No, cheesecake. _____ sweet. I hope you like it.

Jie: Everything looks great. _____ thank your parents after the meal.

Exercise 5: Practise Speaking

☐☐ Practise reading the dialogue with a partner. Then change roles and read it again.

Kinds of Restaurants

Exercise 1: Get Ready to Read

A. Work in a group. Look at the pictures and discuss the answers to these questions.

1. What kind of restaurant do you see in each picture?

2. What are the differences between the two restaurants?

3. What does "fast food" mean? What can you eat in a fast-food restaurant?

4. What does "fine dining" mean? What can you eat in this kind of restaurant?

5. What is an ethnic restaurant? What can you eat in an ethnic restaurant?

B. In your group, look at the list of things you do in different restaurants. For each sentence, write **D** for fine dining, **F** for fast food, and **E** for ethnic. You can write more than one letter for some sentences.

1. You eat at the counter.

2. You have Chinese food.

3. You have wine.

4. You have many courses.

5. You can have spaghetti or pizza.

6. You use plastic cutlery.

7. Your food is well prepared.

8. You eat in a hurry.

9. You celebrate a special occasion.

Exercise 2: Read Carefully for Information

Read the description of three kinds of restaurant. Make a chart similar to the one that follows. Work with a partner to put information from the text on the chart. Put an **X** where you have no information.

Kinds of Restaurants

Canada has many different kinds of restaurants. When you eat out, you have many choices.

Some restaurants have fine dining. The tables have tablecloths on them. The tables are set with many knives, forks, spoons and dishes. There are many items on the menu. You can order wine or other liquors. The food is prepared well and can be expensive. Sometimes the service is very slow. If you want to go out for a special dinner or for a special occasion, it is nice to go to a fancy restaurant.

Fast-food restaurants are the opposite. You eat at a counter or at a small table. The cutlery and dishes are usually made of plastic. Fast-food restaurants are self-service. This means you serve yourself. First you go to the counter and order your food. Then you pay for your food and carry it to a table.

A fast-food restaurant has only a few items on the menu. You can have soft drinks, but there is no wine or liquor. The food is not very expensive. It is a good place to go when you are in a hurry.

Ethnic restaurants are restaurants that have one special kind of food. Most big cities have a variety of ethnic restaurants. The most popular ethnic restaurants are Chinese, Italian, French and Greek. You can also find Vietnamese, Japanese, Indian and Caribbean restaurants.

Some ethnic restaurants have fine dining, others are like fast-food restaurants. Ethnic restaurants can be inexpensive, moderate or expensive. You can eat at a counter or at a table. Sometimes the service is fast, and sometimes it is slow.

	Fine Dining	**Fast Food**	**Ethnic**
Table			
Table setting			
Kind of service			
What you can drink			
Variety of foods			
Price			

Paying the Bill

Listening Activity 16

Exercise 1: Get Ready to Listen

Before you begin, cover Exercise 4 on page 133.

A.   Read this paragraph quickly. Then answer the questions that follow.

At most restaurants, you can pay cash or use a credit card. The waiter brings a bill to the table. Sometimes you pay the waiter. Sometimes you pay at the cash. If you are not sure, you should ask the waiter. At a fast food-restaurant, you must pay cash. You pay for your meal at the counter where you order your food.

1.   What are two ways to pay at a restaurant?

2.   Name two places where you can pay the bill in most restaurants.

3.   Where do you pay in a fast-food restaurant?

B.   Look at the bill below.

1.   Which prices are for food or drink?

2.   Which prices are for tax?

```
-------------------------
Receipt
$22.00 Fish
   3.95
   2.50


   6.20


  34.65 Subtotal


   2.42
   2.77 Provincial Tax


  39.84 Total
-------------------------
```

⬚ Exercise 2: Listen for Meaning

Listen to the conversation on the tape. What is the conversation about?

⬚ Exercise 3: Listen for Details

First, make a bill similar to the one you see. Then, while you listen, write the information that is missing on the bill.

⬚ Exercise 4: Listen for Sounds

While you listen, write the missing words.

Paying the Bill

Customer: Waiter, excuse _____. I don't understand this bill.

Waiter: No problem, sir. I can explain. What don't you understand?

Customer: What is this $22.00 for?

Waiter: That _____ for the fish sir. You and your friend each had fish. The fish is $11.00 each. That comes to $22.00.

Customer: And what's this $3.95 and $2.50? _____ that the wine?

Waiter: No sir. That's the desserts.

Customer: Oh. Which _____ the cheesecake?

Waiter: The cheesecake is $3.95. The apple pie is $2.50.

Customer: What about this $6.20?

Waiter: That's _____ the wine. Your total bill comes _____ $34.65 with the wine.

134

Customer: But the bill says $39.84

Waiter: I ____ explain. You have to add on 7 percent GST and 8 percent provincial tax.

Customer: GST?

Waiter: GST. Goods and Services Tax, sir. It's added to everything.

Customer: Oh, really. The food was good, but I ____ like the tax in Canada!

Waiter: I agree. Nobody likes paying taxes!

Exercise 5: Practise Speaking

Practise reading the dialogue with a partner. Then change roles and read it again.

Supplementary Grammar

Demonstrative Pronouns

This, that, these and **those** are demonstrative pronouns.

This and
That
are singular

This means something near.
That means something far.

These and
Those
are plural.

These means some things that are near.
Those means some things that are far.

Exercise 1

Find the sentences with errors in them. Write the sentences out correctly.

1. These class is already full.
2. This books were open.
3. That news was funny.
4. These marks are low.
5. Those students will fail.
6. That teacher is nice.
7. Give me those pencil.
8. I like this course.
9. That dictionary is the best.

Exercise 2

Write five sentences using **this, that, these** and **those** correctly.

Exercise 3

Change singular to plural and plural to singular in these sentences.

1. I don't like this person.
2. People usually remember those names.
3. These names are popular.
4. Those countries are far away.
5. This student is Swiss.
6. I like that country.
7. That form is too long.
8. Those questions are strange.
9. This name is spelled wrong.
10. These are Japanese customs.

The Present Continuous in Contrast to the Present Simple

Usage

The present simple tense is for actions that are **usual** and **permanent**:

> Birds fly.
> Fish swim.
> Humans think.

It is also used for actions that are **habitual**:

> I walk to school.
> I wake up at 7:30.

The present continuous aspect is for actions that are not yet complete or finished. It is often used with the adverbs "now" or "at present," or with defined times like "this week" or "this year."

> He is watching TV.
> She is sleeping right now.
> They are looking for an apartment.

Exercise 1

Choose the present simple or the present continuous form of the verb in these sentences about moving to a new place. Write the sentences out.

1. Many people _____ (look) for apartments in the spring.
2. Families sometimes _____ (move) across town.
3. It's September, and many students _____ (look) for apartments.
4. I can see some students now. They _____ (move) their furniture into a building.
5. Mr. and Mrs. Lin _____ (try) to find an apartment quickly.
6. Students sometimes _____ (share) an apartment.
7. Look at the neighbours. They _____ (carry) a new couch into the house.
8. The man you see there _____ (buy) a lamp from Mauricio.
9. In North America, pets often _____ (live) in people's houses.
10. Ralph isn't here. He _____ (take) his dog for a walk.

Exercise 2

Write three sentences about students and the things they usually do. Then write three sentences about people in the class and what they are doing now.

Exercise 3

Choose the present simple or the present continuous form of the verb in these sentences about the English class. Write the sentences out.

1. The students in this class usually _____ (arrive) on time.
2. This teacher always _____ (make) the class interesting.
3. Pay attention, Alejandra. The teacher _____ (talk).
4. The class _____ (start) now.
5. The teacher _____ (give) us instructions.
6. Wait. I _____ (look for) my pencil.
7. Look. That group _____ (talk about) the answers.
8. Simon is absent. Maybe he _____ (sleep).
9. Those students _____ (arrive) late nearly every day.
10. It's quiet. The students _____ (write) an exam.

Possessive Adjectives

Formation

The following chart shows the form of singular and plural possessive adjectives.

my	our
your	your
his	
her	their
its	

The nouns that follow possessive adjectives can be singular or plural.

Examples:

her friend	her friends
his aunts	their aunts

Usage

The adjectives in these sentences show possession:

This is **my** apartment. (I live here.)

This is **our** house. (My family and I live here.)

This is **your** class. (This is Lin's class.)

That is **your** school. (Lin, Reiko and Alvaro study here.)

This is **his** aunt. (John's aunt)

This is **her** aunt. (Maria's aunt)

The blackboard is in **its** place. (It is at the front of the classroom.)

The students like **their** teacher. (They all have the same teacher.)

Exercise 1

Choose the best adjective for each sentence. Write the sentences out.

1. I'm homesick because I miss (my, your) family.
2. Tanya and I met (her, our) classmates at the movie.
3. Mrs. James likes (his, her) job at the hospital.
4. Mr. and Mrs. Lin are happy with (its, their) new house.
5. (Our, its) country is very big.

6. Peter met (their, his) brother in the street.

7. Alvaro and Mauricio don't like to clean (their, its) apartment.

8. Mr. Billard works at (its, his) desk.

9. (Our, your) families usually give us good advice.

10. Tara's clothes are not in (its, their) place.

Exercise 2

Choose the correct adjective for each sentence. Write the sentences out.

my   our   your   his   her   its   their

1. Ria and Gaby live in Ottawa. _____ apartment is small.

2. Ray and I bought some furniture. _____ furniture is second-hand.

3. Canada got a new flag in 1967. _____ flag is red and white.

4. I got married last year. _____ husband is French.

5. Mrs. James wants a good school for _____ son.

6. You understand this question. Can you show me _____ answer?

7. The students really like _____ teacher.

8. Mr. Windsor put the chalk in _____ pocket.

9. I can't find _____ dictionary.

10. My father wants my sister and me to live with _____ aunt in Canada.

Can: Ability and Permission

Can is a modal auxiliary verb.

Formation

Can is an auxiliary verb. It goes before the main verb:

My aunt can swim well.

The weather can change quickly here.

Question Formation

To make a question, use the auxiliary verb **can** followed by the subject. Look at this example:

The teacher can speak Japanese.

Can you speak English?

Negative Form

To use **can** in the negative, add **not**. Look at the example:

    We can speak French.

    We cannot speak English.

Usage

Can is used in two ways:

1. To give the idea of ability:

    He can swim.

2. To give the idea of permission:

    You can leave early.

In the negative, the contraction is **can't**.

"Can" for Ability

Exercise 1

Make questions from these statements.

1. Richard can speak Indonesian.

2. That plane can cross the Atlantic Ocean in six hours.

3. I can pass that exam.

4. A dog can run faster than a person.

5. Olga can speak five languages.

6. Mika can cook Japanese food very well.

7. Charles can eat more than Geoff.

8. You can take the bus to school from your house.

Exercise 2

Make these sentences negative.

1. We can understand Gaby's accent.

2. We can get hamburgers in that restaurant.

3. Ray Pinto can speak French very well.

4. The weather can change 20 degrees in one day.

5. Tourists can ski in Indonesia.

6. The president can speak Spanish.

7. It can snow in very cold weather.

8. We can walk to school.

Exercise 3

Make a chart similar to the one below. Ask students in the class for the information you need to fill it in.

	Student's Name	Yes	No
Speak French	Gaby	✔	
Walk to school			
Ski			
Cook very well			
Swim well			
Play tennis			
Play music			

Now write sentences about your classmates. Use the information on the chart. Use **can**.

Example: Gaby can speak French.

"Can" for Permission

Exercise 1

Make questions from these statements.

1. I can ask a question now.

2. He can leave the room now.

3. Cora can use your pencil all day.

4. You can use their phone.

5. We can leave by this door.

6. The students can listen again now.

7. We can meet later.

Exercise 2

Make negative sentences from the statements above. Then complete the sentences using a clause beginning with **but**.

Example:

You can't ask a question now but you can ask later.

Exercise 3

Make two lists. Make one of things you can do in the class. Make another of things you can't do in the class.

Making Questions

You ask a question by changing the place of the subject and verbs.

He is hungry.

Is he hungry?

The answer will be "yes" or "no."

You can add a question word if you want more information.

Is he hungry?

Why is he hungry?

The answer will be, "He didn't eat breakfast."

Exercise 1

Match the question words to the answers:

Question Words	Answers
why	at 6 o'clock
when	by train
where	in Vancouver
what	your brother
who	because I'm tired
how	my suitcase

Exercise 2

Write the questions.

Exercise 3

Write six questions to ask you partner about his or her life.

Adverbs of Frequency

These adverbs are used before the main verb in a sentence:

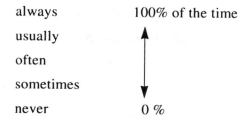

always	100% of the time
usually	
often	
sometimes	
never	0 %

Examples:

In China we **always** eat rice with our meals.

They **usually** set the table at 5:30.

Exception: when the main verb is **to be**:

Mexicans are **often** happy to taste chili sauce.

The adverbs **sometimes**, **usually** and **often** can be used to begin a sentence.

Examples:

Sometimes we eat dinner at noon on Sunday.

Usually Indonesians prefer rice with their meals.

Often children go to school without breakfast.

Exercise 1

Write **C** (correct) or **W** (wrong) for each sentence. Correct sentences that use adverbs of frequency in the wrong place.

1. We sometimes eat salad without salad dressing.

2. Europeans eat never their meals without bread.

3. Canadians usually are too busy to eat lunch.

4. Always my aunt uses onions in her cooking.

5. Pancakes are often served for breakfast.

6. Sometimes we eat dinner at 7 o'clock.

7. My secretary always feels hungry in the middle of the morning.

8. Never Canadians eat hot sauces with their meals.

9. This restaurant is usually very good.

Exercise 2

Write the sentences with the adverbs in the correct place.

1. A Canadian has juice with breakfast. (often)

2. Bread is served with meals in Europe. (usually)

3. I add salad dressing to my salad. (never)

4. Potatoes and corn are cooked. (always)

5. Carrots are served raw in Canada. (sometimes)

6. Oil and vinegar are used in salad dressing. (usually)

7. Rice is a good thing to serve to Vietnamese friends. (always)

8. We cook green peppers before we serve them. (sometimes)

9. Chicken is a popular food at an international dinner. (usually)

10. Canadians eat bread. (often)

Exercise 3

Write five sentences about foods that you like to eat. Use an adverb of frequency in each sentence.

The Simple Past Tense

Formation

To form the simple past tense add **-ed** to the verb:

you answer

you answered

Some irregular verbs have the same form in the present and past:

put

hit

cost

cut

spread

shut

read (note that the pronunciation changes in the past tense to "red")

Many irregular verbs have a different form in the present and past:

write	wrote
say	said
stand	stood
go	went
give	gave
take	took

For a more complete list of irregular past tense verbs see page 149.

Usage

You use the simple past for an action that was completed in past time:

I wrote a letter this morning.

He walked to school yesterday.

Exercise 1

Give the past tense of the following verbs:

1. give	12. call
2. think	13. feel
3. write	14. build
4. follow	15. eat
5. teach	16. cost
6. understand	17. sell
7. know	18. drink
8. see	19. put
9. take	20. buy
10. speak	21. wear
11. find	

Exercise 2

Write out the sentences. Use the correct form of the past tense.

1. We _____ (go) to a movie last night.

2. The students _____ (watch) a movie.

3. Nobody _____ (know) the answer.

4. The hamburger _____ (cost) less than $2.

5. My friend _____ (call) me last night.

6. The subway_____ (take) longer than we expected.

7. We _____ (drink) a cup of coffee after the movie.

8. We _____ (listen) to a really nice song.

9. Roberto _____ (pay) for Janet's lunch.

10. Three students _____ (come) to the party last night.

Exercise 3

Write five sentences about coffee in the simple past tense. Use these verbs:

come   begin   drink   eat   became

Question Formation

To make a question in the simple past tense, use the subject and the past form of the auxiliary verb **do**. The past form is **did**.

Children **walked** to school.

Did children **walk** to school?

The people **ate** in a restaurant.

Did the people **eat** in a restaurant?

When the auxiliary verb **did** is in the past, the main verb is not in the past. Look at another example:

They **went** to an expensive restaurant.

Did they **go** to an expensive restaurant?

Exercise 1

Read these questions. Find the sentences that are correct. Correct the sentences that are wrong.

1. Did the waiter served the food?
2. Did people need dessert after the meal?
3. Did business executives visited Tokyo often?
4. Did everyone ate rice with the meal?
5. Did the meal take a long time?
6. Did the customers left a tip?
7. Did many people ordered fish yesterday?

Exercise 2

Make questions in the simple past tense from these statements.

1. The customers paid at the table.
2. We visited that restaurant often.
3. The father cut and served the meat.
4. Kim wanted to try the dessert.
5. They went to the restaurant by car.
6. They finished the salad quickly.
7. Waiters carried the food on trays.
8. They took a long time to cook the meal.
9. I asked for the bill.
10. People had a good time.

Negative Form

To make the simple past tense negative, use the past form of the auxiliary **do**, and add **not**. The past form is **did**.

We **went** to a French restaurant.

We did not **go** to a Greek restaurant.

When the auxiliary verb **do** is in the past, the main verb is not in the past. Look at another example:

They **ordered** the same meal.

They did not **order** the same drink.

The contraction of the negative form in the past tense is **didn't**.

Exercise 1

Make these sentences negative. You can use the contraction **didn't**.

1. Our guests arrived on time.
2. The waiter brought the bill.
3. The owner came to meet us at the door.
4. The cook came to the table.
5. The restaurant served wine.
6. It took a long time to finish the meal.
7. My aunt understood the menu very well.
8. We enjoyed the meal.
9. My sister had dessert.

Exercise 2

Write five sentences in the simple past. Use **did not.**

Irregular Past Tense Verbs

become	became
begin	began
bring	brought
build	built
buy	bought
come	came
cost	cost
cut	cut
drink	drank
eat	ate
fall	fell
feel	felt
find	found
forget	forgot
give	gave
go	went
get	got

grow	grew
have	had
hear	heard
know	knew
leave	left
lose	lost
make	made
pay	paid
put	put
read	read*
ride	rode
run	ran
see	saw
sell	sold
send	sent
sit	sat
sleep	slept
speak	spoke
take	took
teach	taught
tell	told
think	thought
understand	understood
wear	wore
write	wrote

* Note that the pronunciation changes in the past tense to "red."

Community Contact Tasks

In the Community

Task #1

Application Form

Where do you think you could find an application form? Some possible places would be a bank, a fitness club or a tourist bureau.

Find an application form. Fill it in. Then bring the application form to class. Compare the information asked for on your form with other application forms.

In the Community

Task #2

Using the Telephone Book

In the white pages of the telephone book, names are listed like this:

Family name	Initial
Nguyen	T
OR	
Family Name	**First Name**
Weston	Elizabeth

Names are listed in alphabetical order. Barker comes before Martin because **B** is before **M** in the alphabet. Elizabeth Weston is listed before Francis Weston, because **E** is before **F** in the alphabet.

When three names begin with the same letter, they follow the order of the second letter in each name.

Example:

Simpson

Stevens

Svensen

A. Look in the telephone book. Find your family name. Answer these questions.

1. How many people have the same family name as you have?

2. Does anyone have your family name and your first name?

3. Does anyone have your family name and your initials?

4. Did you look in the white pages or the yellow pages?

B. Look up three common family names. Answer these questions.

1. How many people can you count with these names? ·

2. How many people with these last names have the first names John or Mary?

In the Community

Task #3

Telephoning

Make a list of the names of the students in your class. Put the list in alphabetical order. Ask the student after you on the list for his or her telephone number.

The student before you on the list will phone you with a message. Phone the student who comes after you on the list, and give him or her the same message.

Write the message that you receive and bring it to class.

In the Community

Task #4

The Furniture Task

Imagine that you have a new apartment. You have $700 to buy furniture. Check prices in a furniture store or the furniture department of a department store. Compare these prices with second-hand furniture prices. Look at the bulletin board at the supermarket or in the newspaper under Used Furniture or Garage Sales.

Complete a chart similar to the one below. Then decide which are the best pieces of furniture to buy for $700.

Furniture	New	Second-hand
Bed		
Table		
Chair		

In the Community

Task #5

The Public Transportation Task

Find out about how to use the public transportation system in your city or in the city or town closest to where you live.

1. Who did you ask?
   a) the bus driver
   b) a Canadian friend
   c) a classmate
   d) other

2. How much do you pay for each of the following?
   a) cash fare
   b) tickets or tokens
   c) a pass

3. Can you transfer:
   a) between buses?
   b) from bus to subway?
   c) from subway to bus?

4. How long is a transfer valid?

5. What time does the transportation system start in the morning?

6. What time does the transportation system close at night?

7. How many seats does the bus have?

8. How do you open the door?
   a) push a gate
   b) push the door
   c) stand on the step

9. What colour are the buses?

10. What does the bus driver wear?
    a) a hat
    b) a tie
    c) a jacket
    e) a blue shirt

In the Community

Task #6

The Supermarket Task

You are inviting three friends to your apartment for dinner. You want to cook a nice meal. You have $50 to spend. Go to the supermarket to check prices. Bring in your menu, with lists of ingredients you will need. Write the price beside each thing you need to buy.

Example: 2 packages of noodles $2.79

In the Community

Task #7

The Weather Task

Check the weather report every day for two weeks.

Week 1

Look for the weather report in the newspaper. Fill in a chart similar to the one on page 159.

Week 2

Listen to the weather report on the radio in the evening or early in the morning. Fill in your chart.

In class, compare the information in your chart with the other students' charts.

Week 1

	Sun	Cloud	Rain	Snow	Wind	High Temperature	Low Temperature
Sunday							
Monday							
Tuesday							
Wednesday							
Thursday							
Friday							
Saturday							

Week 2

	Sun	Cloud	Rain	Snow	Wind	High Temperature	Low Temperature
Sunday							
Monday							
Tuesday							
Wednesday							
Thursday							
Friday							
Saturday							

Englisch ist einfach

私は英語が好きです.

اللغة الإنجليزية سهلة

Saya suka buku ini

Bu Kitapi cok scudim

See you in Canadian Concepts 3 !

我會說英文

မင်္ဂလာပါ

Mi piace molto questo libro

Tôi thích quyển sách này

Inglês é fácil de aprender.

Je parle l'anglais

안녕

Mijaw Ejɔuwuò

さようなら
私は、この本から
たくさんの英語を学びました。

Me gusta este libro